Additional Praise

Future of E...

"This book makes a strong case that generative AI models are more than obstacles for educators to work around, and that if used thoughtfully and creatively, they can help teachers and administrators prepare their students to thrive in a rapidly changing technological environment. Shah understands that using AI in our classrooms won't come naturally to most of us, and offers concrete suggestions throughout, ranging from useful tips for modifying traditional assignments all the way to insightful recommendations for reimagining what the aims of formal education ought to be in the first place."

—**Jeff Behrends,** Senior Research Scholar,
Department of Philosophy, Harvard University

"Priten Shah's knowledge, experience, and spirit of public service in the fields of AI and education make this book essential reading for educators at all levels. He offers a must-read for teachers, administrators, parents, and policymakers on the voyage to best practices for using AI in classrooms."

—**Anne L'Hommedieu-Sanderson,** Executive Director,
ThinkerAnalytix and Associate of the Department
of Philosophy, Harvard University

"While teaching in the age of artificial intelligence may be intimidating for some, Shah's cogent and concise book is a great asset for educators, administrators, and school boards. *AI and the Future of Education* can especially help teachers better understand and incorporate the possibilities of AI as they continue to keep students at the center of all they do."

—**Ajay Nair, PhD,** President, Arcadia University

"The depth of Priten Shah's background in education and tech, and the clarity of his thinking and writing, make *AI and the Future of Education* a first-rate introduction to the subject. He offers a framework for understanding the basics of programs like ChatGPT, and his recommendations will offer excellent guidance to teachers and leaders in their exploration and evaluation of these tools, helping them to navigate the radical change that AI is already bringing to education."

—Bill Wharton, former Head of School,
The Commonwealth School

AI AND THE
FUTURE OF EDUCATION

AI AND THE FUTURE OF EDUCATION

Teaching in the Age of Artificial Intelligence

PRITEN SHAH

JB JOSSEY-BASS™

A Wiley Brand

Published by John Wiley & Sons, Inc., Hoboken, New Jersey.
Published simultaneously in Canada.

For general information on our other products and services or for technical support,
please contact our Customer Care Department within the United States at (800) 762-
2974, outside the United States at (317) 572-3993 or fax (317) 572-4002.

Wiley also publishes its books in a variety of electronic formats. Some content that
appears in print may not be available in electronic formats. For more information about
Wiley products, visit our web site at www.wiley.com.

Library of Congress Cataloging-in-Publication Data is Available:

ISBN 9781394219247 (Paperback)
ISBN 9781394219261 (ePDF)
ISBN 9781394219254 (ePUB)

COVER DESIGN: PAUL MCCARTHY
COVER ART: © SHUTTERSTOCK | BLUE HOUSE STUDIO

SKY10069696_031424

Contents

Preface

This book is meant to provide an introduction to educators who are interested in learning about both the current and future capabilities of artificial intelligence (AI) in education. It focuses primarily on generative artificial intelligence (popularized by ChatGPT, Google's Bard, and Microsoft's Bing Chat), and offers teachers concrete insight into how they can use these technologies now and how they will likely be able to use them in the near future.

AI is rapidly developing, and the book aims to be independent of a particular snapshot in time by offering relevant advice at multiple stages of AI development. It does not assume that AI will remain incapable of a particular skill set, and it sets the stage for the large-scale changes that will be necessary in the coming years.

I highly encourage you to read all the prompt suggestions in every chapter, or at least skim through them, as the prompts (Chapter 2 explains this further) offer insight into effectively using these AI systems in your classroom. In that way, the book is meant to be a practical primer and does not focus on capabilities that teachers cannot yet use (e.g., sentiment analysis of facial expressions) and provides tips that are actionable immediately.

You will want to try at least some of the prompts from each section, and remember to add more context about the subject you're teaching, the age group, any standards or learning objectives you have, and what output you are seeking. I have limited the prompts in size to help you quickly see the possibilities, and Chapter 2 explains how to write the most effective prompts.

Both to acknowledge the rapid pace of development and to keep the length manageable, I have limited the focus on content specific to a particular model, tool, or platform. I hope to allow teachers to choose the platform that best suits their needs when they read the book. We provide many more tool guides, lesson plans, prompts, and examples on our website at pedagog.ai, and we encourage you to access those resources as you work through the book.

Of course, a logical question most readers will ask is: "Did AI write this book?" While AI did not write the book, it was used to help prepare it. The book was, however, ultimately written, edited, and put together by a team of real humans. Various AI tools, including some of our own implementations, such as OpenAI's ChatGPT, Google's Bard, and Microsoft's Bing Chat, were consulted throughout the book as brainstorming buddies, thought partners, and a second pair of eyes on a funky-sounding paragraph. To help illustrate the role that AI can play in our workflow, the following lists the prompts used:

Prompt: "These are the guiding questions I'm considering discussing in a book section on the future of education and AI on {fill}. Are there any questions that seem unclear or irrelevant to this section?"

Prompt: "I'm trying to create an example for teachers on {fill}. This is what I have so far {fill}. What else could I add to provide a thorough picture?"

Prompt: "You are a prompt generator that helps me generate a prompt for teachers to use in generative AI tools so that they can do {fill}. What prompt would you use?"

Prompt: "This is a paragraph in a book on AI and the future of education. Provide me with suggestions for what you would change to ensure teachers can understand it properly: {fill}."

AI tools were also used to help edit the manuscript, where particular suggestions were provided, and I modified my grammatical structure or word choice based on their insight. Grammarly's AI-powered grammar and spell check system helped me rapidly review work and correct typos or errors.

As you read the book, you'll notice that most sections include big-picture insights into what changes can and might look like and more accessible information on how to approach AI for various uses. I encourage you to focus on both so you can see where we are headed and are prepared to navigate teaching in the age of AI.

Chapter 1

Embracing AI in Education

In response to the rapid development of artificial intelligence (AI), during the 2022–2023 school year, educators voiced concerns over plagiarism, cheating, and the futility of many of their traditional assignments. Suddenly, within minutes, students could generate essays that were hard to tell apart from human writing. Conventional plagiarism detection methods became obsolete as generative AI produced individual responses for each student. Some teachers scrambled to modify their assignments to keep up with the changes, while others were unaware of the newfound technological developments.

While the issue of academic integrity was pertinent in the months following the advent of these new technologies, the longer-term conversation must involve embracing and making room for AI to ensure our classrooms meet our students' needs effectively. Educators must learn what AI is, how students are using and can use it, how it can make their lives easier, and how pedagogical goals that once seemed impossible can now be reached.

This book is a primer for educators to do just that. Throughout the chapters, I provide background information on the technological changes (both past, present, and likely future) and what that means for every teacher across the educational system. In addition, the book contains examples, tips and tricks, and thought-provoking questions to help prepare educators to teach in the age of AI.

Significant technological developments have always forced educators and the systems they work in to evolve to meet the educational needs of their students and take advantage of new opportunities. In that way, AI is similar to the challenges that educators have faced in the past. However, what makes these challenges different is the rapid pace at which they are developing, and the pain points and fractures within our educational models that they are exposing. These two factors make it essential that educators think about the implications of these developments on their practice and pedagogy quicker and more thoroughly than ever before.

To help educators do just that, Chapter 2 helps teachers develop a fundamental understanding of what AI is and how it is related to education, Chapter 3 highlights the fractures created by AI and identifies opportunities for large-scale change and adaptation in education, and Chapter 4 helps adapt traditional pedagogical theory to AI.

While plagiarism and academic integrity may have captured the initial public dialogue for education, I hope to present a more optimistic future for education. If these technologies are integrated and adapted to, instead of fought and avoided, educators and students will be better equipped for the world that awaits us as AI revolutionizes our societies.

OPPORTUNITIES AND CHALLENGES: AI IN THE CLASSROOM

- What opportunities does AI present in the classroom?
- What challenges do educators face when implementing AI?
- What are the risks of overreliance on AI in the classroom?

While AI has intruded upon our classrooms, the opportunities it will create for our schools far outweigh the risks such technologies pose. The transition and adaptation will not be seamless, as we've already started to see, but with the proper knowledge and skills, educators can approach this new age ready to focus on what they do best: teach our students. Nonetheless, as with any rapid development, we must carefully consider how, when, and why we shift our practice and pedagogy in response to AI. While the entirety of this book is devoted to helping teachers carefully navigate this transition, the following sections provide an overview of the opportunities and challenges that AI is bringing.

The Opportunities

In the wake of the COVID-19 pandemic, teacher burnout and attrition were at all-time highs. This was not surprising given the growing blend of challenges teachers face. They are suffering from the pedagogical challenges of students who are academically behind, disengaged with the classroom, and presenting with various developmental, cognitive, and socioemotional needs. In addition, they are burdened by the practical challenges of keeping up with parent and administrative communication, implementing multiple systems and protocols, and ensuring they generate standards-aligned material. These have combined to push teachers to the breaking point and caused a nationwide teacher shortage. While AI cannot fill in the gaps created in the classroom by our departing colleagues, it can help solve and mitigate many of these challenges and make teaching a less daunting experience for current and future teachers.

Teachers spend countless hours outside their instructional time planning lessons and activities, preparing instructional materials, providing assessment feedback, and managing administrative tasks. These tasks are independent of teachers' face-to-face time with students, and involve generating and responding to content for various non-instructional purposes. The development of generative AI technology thus offers a path to offloading much of the workload that happens behind the scenes of instructional time. AI can help outline curriculum, draft lesson plans, generate assessments, and draft communication and feedback for teachers. The more teachers can rely on AI for this portion of their workload, the more time and energy they will have to focus on providing students with direct instruction. Chapters 5 and 6 provide suggestions for educators on how to best use AI tools to make their own time more effective and valuable.

AI can also solve many of our pedagogical problems by providing us with custom, individualized, technology-based solutions to the issues we are facing. Creating personalized, interactive, and dynamic learning opportunities is becoming easier and more accessible for a broader range of educators to meet our students where they are and help keep them engaged in the learning process. Recent developments in AI technology will allow teachers to tailor their instruction and assignments to individual students, creating a more equitable and effective teaching strategy. In addition, AI systems will be able to help teachers analyze student data, and pinpoint learning difficulties and gaps quicker to provide targeted support for struggling students. Chapter 7 details how educators can use AI to boost student differentiation and engagement through various strategies and tools.

Many of these opportunities are already present with the technologies as they stand now, and in the upcoming years, these will only further develop and present more ways for teachers to shift how they spend their time.

The Challenges

As educators begin to take advantage of these opportunities, it will remain essential to engage critically about how much we come to rely on these technologies. There are significant ethical and practical challenges that such drastic changes in our workflow and pedagogical tools will bring, and both students and teachers need to be able to think and act critically.

As students prepare to enter a world where AI is ubiquitous, whether in future educational stages, their careers, or their social lives, they will need to be able to analyze the ethical and social implications of various AI technologies. They will have to be able to navigate how and when to use the assistance of AI and define what integrity means for them and their peers. As democratic participation and dialogue change, students must be able to navigate misinformation, deepfake media, and tailored manipulation and propaganda. They will also need to think through what they produce and put out into the world and its consequences for the rest of society. Finally, they will have to critically evaluate the output of AI to spot and address biases and inaccuracies. Chapter 8 provides guidance on critical skills and dispositions students will need to develop in school to successfully navigate these challenges later in life.

Educators, too, will need to act carefully to ensure that introducing AI doesn't worsen existing problems in education. While AI has the potential to help us narrow the achievement gap, we need to ensure that our responses take advantage of it to do so rather than risk widening it. To do so, we will also need to make progress on closing the digital divide to ensure that AI's benefits are equitable. Finally, as more data and information is shared with AI companies and providers, educators need to be able to think through data privacy and security to ensure that students are not exploited for profit gains. Some initial thinking and background on these issues are covered in Chapter 9.

Given the nature of technological developments and AI specifically, teachers will need to focus on self-evaluating their skills and knowledge to navigate these challenges. While teachers do not have to become technical experts in machine learning, there are core skills and knowledge that will help them navigate the age of AI. They will also have to constantly remain in tune with new developments and progress and seek resources that help build on their practice. In fact, teachers can turn to AI itself for their own professional and personal development. All of these suggestions are built upon in Chapter 10.

Risks

One of the fears echoing from most industries is about the future of the workforce in the age of AI. Educators, however, will remain crucial players in helping prepare students for the future world. At the same time, the drastic increase in reliance on technology brings risks that we must balance.

While I have outlined how AI can enhance instruction, educators must balance technology and face-to-face interactions to maintain the essential human element in education. These interactions are critical for fostering empathy, social skills, and emotional intelligence. We must continue to advocate for the importance of educators as human facilitators of knowledge and skill acquisition. Most of the book is devoted to helping teachers adapt to this role.

Educators must also be careful because an excessive focus on AI in the classroom may lead to an unhealthy dependence on technology, diminishing students' ability to think critically and solve problems without digital assistance. While just like the calculator and even the smartphone have changed what kinds of skills students need in order to function effectively in the world, higher-level skills are built on lower-level ones, and moving too quickly away from them can risk students who are unable to work independently. The strategies outlined in this book are designed to ensure that students continue to learn the fundamental skills necessary for the rest of their lives while still developing fluency with the tools and systems they will encounter throughout their lives.

These risks are not so great that we should avoid or fear the introduction of AI, but they are significant enough that they warrant thoughtful implementation and integration strategies. The following section offers a framework for thinking about how we integrate AI into our educational systems.

SUSTAINABLE AI INTEGRATION STRATEGIES

- What are the key components of successful AI integration?
- What are implementation strategies that will work long term?
- What are bridges to future implementation strategies?

It is not an easy task to integrate AI into our educational systems. While individual teachers and students across the country are already exploring ways to connect AI with their pedagogical and educational goals, a sustainable strategy will be necessary in order to avoid knee-jerk reactions that either risk exposing students to technology that isn't ready for the classroom or leave them far behind their peers. While many of these strategies will be at the district and state level, teachers will likely have to adapt faster than these institutions work and play a crucial role in helping policymakers craft the right strategies.

Before starting to think about integrating AI into your classroom, it will be helpful to outline the goals, timelines, and purpose of doing so. This will create a vision from which you can choose how to evaluate tools, help you make curricular decisions, and guide your conversations with other stakeholders. Here are some questions you can ask yourself:

- What are my overall educational objectives for incorporating AI in the classroom?
  - What problems am I trying to solve?
  - What standards am I trying to meet?
  - What do I want my students to gain from the integration?
- What are important events around which I can plan my integration?
  - Are there semesters or quarters I can divide my plan into?
  - Are there particular units or chapters where I have more leeway to try new things?
  - How much time will I need to introduce the concepts or tools to my students?
- What am I trying to solve with AI integration?
  - Am I integrating so my students don't fall behind?
  - Am I integrating to better meet my already established pedagogical goals?
  - Am I integrating to make my life easier and allow me to focus on teaching?

- Are there real-world skills I want to ensure my students gain from this experience?

Once you have your big-picture view, consider what outside support or involvement you'll need to make these goals a reality. Here are some questions to think about which stakeholders need to be involved and what role they have to play:

- What administrators' buy-in do you need? Are there district policies to navigate or change?
- What other teachers should you involve? Are they interdisciplinary connections you can make across departments?
- What is the sentiment from your students? Are they asking questions or already using AI?
- How involved is your parent population? What will their perception be?
- What level of training and support will you need from your district, and what will you be able to seek yourself?

Once you know what role others will play in your integration, it is time to consider the practical considerations of how you will go about your plan. You need to think through the details about tools, data, and implementation. Here are some questions to guide that:

- What specific tasks or responsibilities would I like to offload to AI?
  - Which tools can help me do those tasks closest in quality to how I would?
- What aspects of my students' learning journey can AI tools support or improve?
  - Which tools are built specifically for that?

- Are there tools that will work across units and for multiple different uses that will save onboarding time?
- How can I ensure that AI tools and technologies are ethically and responsibly used in my classroom?
  - What guidelines or policies should be in place to help my students navigate the new technology?
- What feedback and data will I rely on to see if my integration works?
  - Are there student or parent surveys I need to prepare?
  - Are there pre- and post-exams, or cross-unit analyses I can do?
- What data and privacy questions do I need to ask?
  - What data is used by the AI company, and how?
  - What student privacy standards does the company have?
  - What policies do they follow, and which ones do my district or school require technology companies to follow?
- Where and when will my students access these tools?
  - Can I ensure access is equitable for all my students?
  - Do the tools have the accessibility features that my students need?

By reflecting on these questions, you can create a clear vision and plan for incorporating AI into your classroom. As you begin to implement AI tools and strategies, be prepared to adapt and refine your approach based on feedback, student outcomes, and new insights from the field of AI in education. You'll have to remember that integrating AI into the classroom is an ongoing process, and your answers to some of these questions might change as you gain experience and the technology continues to develop.

As you work through this book, you will gain insight and knowledge to help you answer these questions, so use them as a starting point for planning your integration strategy.

When answering these questions, consider how your investment in acquiring this knowledge can be helpful long term. AI is not a short-term fad; your investments now should help you prepare for future developments. No one is certain where AI technology is headed in the next few years, so teachers have to ensure that as they embrace these changes, they are preparing themselves for lifelong learning, both for themselves and their students.

Standards, institutional assessments, expectations, and the workforce will drastically differ within your career span. Therefore, your short-term goal will be to create fluency for yourself and your students with these changes such that you can quickly adapt and implement any changes that policymakers make.

Overcoming Barriers to AI Adoption

- What resistance will educators and policymakers have to AI-driven change in education?

- What resistance will parents and students have to AI-driven change in education?

- How can educators overcome resistance to AI adoption, and promote understanding and acceptance of generative AI technology in the classroom?

After you have crafted your strategy and goals, you will have to consider external pressures against your implementation. We already see a negative backlash to AI in some schools, with many major districts implementing bans and policies against AI. Educators and the general public are vocalizing a lot more concerns about AI. If the integration of AI technology is to be successful, it is crucial to address the various concerns these stakeholders may have.

While bans on AI in education may provide a short-term solution, they are not a long-term strategy for addressing the challenges of the rapidly evolving educational landscape. As AI technologies continue to advance and become more prevalent, educators will need to be prepared to show examples of successful AI integration in education and preemptively answer questions and concerns from stakeholders.

Thus, to effectively implement AI in their classrooms, it will be necessary for educators to be proactive in addressing concerns and promoting understanding and acceptance of AI technology. By sharing success stories and answering questions from stakeholders, educators can help build support for AI integration in education and ensure that students are well-prepared for the rapidly evolving technological landscape.

Educators and policymakers may resist AI-driven change due to fears of job security or insufficient training and support. Limited budgets and competing priorities may also make investing in AI technology and related professional development challenging for schools and districts.

Resistance to change may also stem from ingrained habits, routines, and traditionalism. Privacy and ethical concerns about data security and bias may also lead to skepticism and hesitation toward AI integration. Additionally, parents and students may have concerns about the potential dehumanization of the classroom, the effectiveness of AI-driven learning experiences compared to traditional teaching methods, and the possible exacerbation of existing educational inequalities.

Educators will have to have the knowledge and experience to communicate against this resistance. Clear communication with stakeholders about the goals, benefits, and potential challenges of AI integration can help build trust and understanding. Involving stakeholders in the decision-making process can also create a sense of ownership and support for AI-driven changes in education. Ongoing education and sharing success stories of AI integration in education can foster greater acceptance and dispel misconceptions. Addressing privacy, ethical, and accessibility concerns proactively can help alleviate fears and build confidence in the use of AI in the classroom.

Ultimately, it's important to emphasize the human element of education and highlight the ways in which AI can enhance, rather than replace, the role of educators. By taking these steps, educators can overcome resistance to AI adoption and promote understanding and acceptance of AI technology in the classroom.

CONCLUSION

In conclusion, integrating AI into education presents significant opportunities and challenges. As we have explored throughout this chapter, AI has the potential to revolutionize teaching and learning by streamlining administrative tasks, enabling personalized learning experiences, and fostering the development of critical skills necessary for success in an increasingly digital world. However, to fully harness these benefits, educators must proactively address concerns and resistance from various stakeholders, including policymakers, parents, and students.

To navigate this rapidly evolving landscape, educators are encouraged to develop a clear vision and strategy for AI integration, engage in ongoing professional development, and remain adaptable to new technologies and approaches. In addition, by fostering open communication, involving stakeholders in the decision-making process, and addressing concerns about privacy, ethics, and accessibility, educators can facilitate the adoption of AI in the classroom and create a more equitable and effective learning environment for their students.

As we move forward, it is essential for educators to stay informed about the latest developments in AI and education and to actively participate in the conversation around its integration. By doing so, they can ensure that they are well-prepared to adapt their teaching practices and pedagogy in response to emerging technologies, ultimately empowering their students to thrive in the ever-evolving world of AI.

Exit Ticket

Start drafting your responses to the questions in the strategies section, and see if you can prepare a letter to your principal asking them to allow you to use specific AI tools in your classroom. Don't worry if you don't have all the necessary information. This is just to get the juices flowing!

Chapter 2

Defining AI

While gaining deep expertise in AI and machine learning is unnecessary for most educators, grasping how the technology works will allow educators to better navigate the age of AI in their classrooms. Many misunderstandings and fears about AI technologies stem from a need to understand the underlying models and the methods used to build them. Knowing how they work will equip you to make effective and ethical use of the technology and understand its limitations and shortcomings.

While particular models and capabilities have recently been attracting attention, AI itself is not a new development and, in fact, already surrounds you in many of your daily interactions. Understanding the broader landscape of the technical concepts surrounding AI will help you see the progression of the technology, and the impact it has and can have on your classroom.

FUNDAMENTALS OF AI AND MACHINE LEARNING

- What are the key concepts and terminology in AI?
- How do AI and machine learning algorithms work?
- What are the different types of machine learning?

Artificial Intelligence refers to the simulation of human intelligence by machines. These include simulations of learning (the acquisition of information and rules for using the information), reasoning (using the rules to reach approximate or definite conclusions), and self-correction (knowing when a mistake has been made and correcting it). In many ways, the job of a computer programmer is very similar to that of an educator! Both help an entity learn, using various methods, and how to think, learn, and behave better.

Within the umbrella term of *artificial intelligence* are multiple theoretical stages that track how much "intelligence" the systems have compared to humans.

Defining Stages of AI

The first stage is the one you've probably seen the most of thus far. Narrow AI (or Weak AI) is designed to perform a narrow task, such as voice recognition, recommendation systems, or image recognition. It operates under a limited context and is not self-aware. You encounter these when you get a suggestion on YouTube for the next video to watch, when you use Siri or Google Assistant, or when you use facial recognition to unlock your phone. These models are trained to perform *particular* tasks like humans. Within this stage are domain-specific AI models where the AI is specifically trained to excel in a particular field. For example, this includes AI systems trained in diagnosing diseases or predicting stock market trends.

Thus far, most computer theorists argue that Narrow AI is the farthest the technology has advanced. However, with the introduction of generative AI systems, like Google's Bard and OpenAI's ChatGPT, there is more of a debate about exactly how close we are to achieving Artificial General Intelligence.

Artificial General Intelligence (or AGI, Strong AI) refers to a type of AI that can understand, learn, adapt, and implement knowledge in a *wide variety of tasks* at the level of a human being. It implies that the AI could perform any intellectual task a human can do.

Anything beyond AGI is referred to as Superintelligent AI, which would surpass human intelligence in practically every field, including scientific creativity, general wisdom, and social skills. This type of AI has yet to exist, and significant debates exist around its feasibility and ethical implications. An important development in Superintelligent AI would be AI that can understand thoughts, emotions, and entities that affect human behavior. The final stage, which is the one that is the premise of many science fiction novels and movies, involves systems that can form representations about themselves. They would have consciousness and self-awareness, similar to human intelligence.

At best, we are currently somewhere between Narrow AI and AGI. Thus, most of this book serves as a practical guide within this context, and while many of the adaptations and practices will be helpful even as AI develops further, the challenges and opportunities will likely evolve.

Building AI Systems

With that understanding of AI, let's turn to how these systems are built and trained. Fundamental to the concept of AI is the concept of machine learning. Therefore, knowing how these models work is vital to understanding the mechanisms of how AI tools are built.

AI systems are built on algorithms that enable computers to learn from data and improve their performance over time. This process is called machine learning. For machine learning to be effective, it needs the proper training data set. The data set is then used to train machine learning algorithms, providing examples from which the model learns patterns and relationships (e.g., what a dog looks like). Based on that training, the system creates a mathematical model representing the relationships and patterns discovered during the learning process, which can be used to make predictions or decisions. When you hear about different AI systems (like GPT-4 and Bard), these are the models they are referring to. They are, in essence, prediction machines in high gear, very similar to how autocomplete works on your phone!

Once data is chosen to train the model (based on its relevance to the type of model being created), researchers will pre-process it by cleaning, transforming, and normalizing it to prepare it for use in the machine learning algorithms. In addition, they will address issues such as missing values, outliers, and inconsistent formatting.

As you can imagine, the quality and quantity of data have huge implications on how well these models perform. The biases, shortcomings, gaps, and flaws in the data are likely to show up in the trained models, and thinking through the potential ways the data is lacking is one way of critically evaluating different models.

Once these models are created, they are deployed into applications or systems to make predictions or decisions based on new, previously unseen data. This is when most users who are not computer scientists will interact with AI systems.

How AI Learns

Earlier, we mentioned that the model is built from machines that use algorithms to learn from the data provided. This process is complicated and can involve one of many different methods used to train the models.

Supervised learning: In supervised learning, algorithms learn from labeled data to make predictions or classifications. For example, a model might be fed thousands of images that are tagged with the animal they contain to train a model to classify future images by which animal is present in the picture. While effective, this model relies on having appropriately labeled data.

Unsupervised learning: In contrast, unsupervised learning uses algorithms that find patterns or structures in unlabeled data. This type of learning is often used when there is no clear idea of what to expect from the data or when the data is so complex that manual labeling would be impractical or impossible. Unsupervised learning algorithms are designed to automatically detect hidden patterns, clusters, or associations within the data. For example, an algorithm might be provided with different books, which must be grouped based on their subjects, reading levels, and languages. A clustering algorithm could analyze all the books, determine which ones are similar based on these characteristics, and group them together.

Unsupervised learning can be further broken down into various types of learning that train the model in different ways.

Reinforcement learning: Reinforcement learning is a type of machine learning where a system learns to behave a certain way by performing actions and observing the results or rewards of those actions. The goal is for it to recognize actions that maximize the reward. For example, reinforcement learning has been used in games where the AI learns to win by playing the game multiple times and improving its strategy based on whether it won or lost previous games. Reinforcement learning can also involve human reinforcement learning, where AI generates output, and then a human grades the output on its quality to help train the model. Many of the most popular generative AI models are built with at least some element of human reinforcement learning.

Deep learning: Deep learning is a subset of machine learning that focuses on algorithms inspired by the structure and function of the brain; these algorithms are called artificial neural networks. These networks are vital components of deep learning algorithms for solving complex tasks. Imagine these networks as a system of stations. There's a starting station (input layer), several middle stations (hidden layers), and a final station (output layer). Each station is connected to all the stations at the next level, just like a well-connected train system. Each station, or "neuron," holds some information. The information moves from the starting station, through the middle stations, and finally to the final station. Along the way, the information gets changed and processed based on rules the system learns from the given data. Deep learning models are designed to automatically learn to represent data by training on large amounts of data, and they are particularly effective at learning patterns from unstructured data such as images, audio, and text. For example, deep learning has automatically translated text into different languages.

Transfer learning: Transfer learning is a method where a pre-trained model (trained for a particular purpose) is used on a new, similar problem. It involves taking a pre-existing trained model for a task and reusing it as the starting point for a different but related assignment. For example, one might train a neural network on a large-scale image classification task, then "tune" the model for another task involving recognizing specific types of objects. The benefit is that it can reduce computational time and improve prediction performance on tasks with limited data by relying on what it learned from the initial task.

Now that you know how most AI models are created, you can see where things might go wrong and what possibilities these models make for education. As you read through this book, you will start to see the direct connection between these concepts and the application of AI in education.

EXPLORING GENERATIVE AI

- What is generative AI, and how does it work?

- What are some current examples of generative AI capabilities?

- What are the implications of generative AI for the future of education?

As of 2022, the realm of AI that had significantly impacted the public sphere was predominantly discriminative AI. This type of AI primarily focuses on classifying and searching information. However, a significant shift in public discourse occurred with the popularization of generative AI, particularly with the public release of models like ChatGPT.

While both generative and discriminative AI rely on many of the same foundational concepts and technologies, their ultimate goals diverge significantly. Discriminative AI seeks to classify and differentiate data, essentially learning the differences between different categories of data. On the other hand, generative AI is designed to create new content or outputs based on the input it receives and its learned understanding of the data provided to its models.

Training generative AI models often involve unsupervised learning, enabling the model to digest and understand large amounts of text, images, or videos. The aim is to identify patterns in how the data is structured or created so that the AI can mimic and replicate it.

Two popular techniques employed in this regard are autoencoding and Generative Adversarial Networks (GANs).

An autoencoder is a neural network that learns to copy its input to its output. Its internal structure allows it to compress the input into a latent-space representation and then reconstruct the output from it. In less technical terms, the model takes the input and simplifies it as much as possible, then recreates it based on the simplified version it had created. This process of learning compressed representations (simplified versions) is beneficial in noise reduction and anomaly detection because the model learns what parts of the input are essential to preserving and which parts are irrelevant. Applied in the context of generative AI, autoencoders can be used to generate new data that shares characteristics with the training data, effectively learning the distribution of the original data and then using the same process it would use to replicate the original to create new content that is similar to the training set.

GANs represent a unique form of generative AI. They involve training two neural networks — a generator and a discriminator — in a competitive setup. The generator's role is to create realistic samples, while the discriminator evaluates the authenticity of these samples. This dual-network competition allows the model to effectively train itself, refining its ability to generate convincing data. This method is particularly prevalent in the creation of image-generative AI models.

The defining characteristic of generative AI is its capacity to produce novel content, designs, and even solutions not present in the original training data. These capabilities of generative AI are vast and continue to expand as more sophisticated models are developed. For example, beyond simple text and image generation, these models can generate high-resolution, realistic images, compose music, write articles, create 3D models, and even generate code.

One of the key features of more recent generative AI tools has been what kinds of input can be used by the model to create output. While many early generative AI models were built to be used within complex systems and applications by computer programmers, models like GPT-4 from OpenAI are directly accessible to the public through a simple natural language interface application like ChatGPT.

The ability for users to talk directly to the AI model has primarily led to widespread usage. Anyone with a computer and internet access can ask a generative AI tool like Google's Bard or Microsoft's Bing Chat to generate unique content for them just by prompting the model. Prompts are the input the user provides the model from which it determines the next step, and more details on effective prompting are provided later in the chapter.

However, the proliferation of generative AI brings with it a unique set of challenges. One of the primary challenges is the quality control of generated content. While generative AI can create high-quality outputs, it can also generate inaccurate or nonsensical results, especially when working outside of the contexts present in the training data. This issue is related to the challenge of AI "hallucination," where the AI generates content that deviates significantly from reality, creating an output based more on the AI's interpretation rather than an accurate representation of the data.

Hallucination is possible because the AI doesn't actually "know" anything and nor does it "think," but rather, at least for now, most of these models are highly effective predictive models that are trained to predict the right combination of words that a human might produce based on the training data it is built with. In practice, this might mean that if the AI model cannot accurately predict or determine the truth value of something (e.g., a historical event), it will provide its best prediction based on the data and not on reality. A large part of the effective use of AI is to quality control the output you receive from AI models.

There are also significant ethical and societal challenges. For example, deep fakes, realistic AI-generated photos, videos, or audio can be used maliciously to spread misinformation or fraud. Plagiarism is another concern, as AI models could potentially generate content that unintentionally resembles copyrighted material. Moreover, AI models can often reflect the biases in their training data, leading to outputs that could perpetuate harmful stereotypes or discrimination. All of these challenges are further explored in later chapters.

Finally, there's the matter of computational and environmental costs. Training large-scale generative AI models requires significant computational resources, leading to high-energy consumption. As the field moves towards more complex and capable models, managing these costs and their environmental impact will be essential. We hope that as the field advances, more efficient solutions are found to avoid significant environmental costs.

Examples of Generative AI

While many generative AI models and tools exist, a few prominent models will appear throughout the book.

Text generation: These models can create coherent and contextually relevant text based on a given prompt. The output is unique, contextually relevant, and can mimic natural human text generation. Popular text generation models include OpenAI's GPT-4, Google's Bard, and Anthropic's Claude. These models will all continue improving their capacity to generate text, whether emails and marketing messages or textbooks and academic papers. For example, these text generation models can already write a catchy slogan for a brand, a personalized email for a customer, or a funny caption for a meme.

Image synthesis: These models generate realistic images, such as faces or objects, using techniques like GANs. Often the output can be customized to be photorealistic, be in the style of a particular artist, or match a specific design style. Popular image generation models include Midjourney, DALL-E 2, and Stable Diffusion. While the capacity to create these images has many creative uses in design and even education, they are also a significant threat to increasing misinformation. For example, these image synthesis models cannot only create a logo for a business or a graphic for a presentation, but also a fake picture of a made-up news event.

Sound processing: These models can both take sound as input and convert it into text, and take text and convert it into spoken speech. Some models produce original music or melodies by learning patterns from existing music, like Google's Magenta project. For example, a speech processing model (like Whisper from OpenAI) can transcribe an online meeting and even take out filler words to make it more readable.

Multi-modal generation: Some models do more than one of these tasks. This expands the potential for their use, especially in professional contexts, as they can handle multiple project parts. For example, tools embedded in Microsoft Office 365 and Canva allow you to generate entire slideshow presentations with text, design, and graphics generated by the AI system.

Implications for Education

At this point, the vast potential for AI in education is becoming apparent, and the rest of the book will continue to explore the implications of generative AI in more concrete and practical ways. However, it is important to start by grouping the implications into a few key areas.

Fundamental purpose: Many of the skills taught in schools are generative ones (writing papers, creating presentations, polishing writing, researching and summarizing expert sources, etc.), and if AI systems can do many of those tasks for our students in the long term, then how do we justify to them, and ourselves, what we are teaching and why we are teaching it the way we have been before the introduction of these technologies.

Content generation: Teachers can use generative AI to create customized learning materials, assessments, presentations, or even entire curricula, saving time and effort in preparing their lessons. They can also have students use AI systems to create projects, help prepare first drafts of papers, and even self-correct assignments with personalized feedback.

Personalized learning: Generative AI can create tailored educational content and resources, adapting to individual student needs and learning styles from the data fed to it. This can be as simple as adjusting a news article to different reading levels. In addition, Generative AI can help make educational resources more accessible by automatically translating, summarizing, or adapting content for diverse student populations.

Ethical considerations: Using generative AI in education raises important ethical questions, such as the potential for replicating biases from flawed data sets or inappropriate content generation. There are also concerns about defining and enforcing academic integrity policies and what it means to produce original work.

While these categories are just meant to prime you for thinking deeper about these implications, we'll explore what they mean in practice in the rest of the book.

EFFECTIVE PROMPT WRITING FOR TEACHERS

- Why is effective prompt writing important for educators using AI?
- What are the key principles for writing effective prompts?
- How can teachers refine and improve their prompt-writing skills?

As previously discussed, some generative AI systems (currently) rely on users prompting them with some sort of input to produce some output. While systems and applications will continue to be built that reduce the amount of prompting or the specificity of the prompting that a user has to do, most popular applications today require users to do a significant amount of careful prompting to produce the desired outputs.

In order to effectively use those AI systems, teachers and students will need to learn how to craft effective prompts that can generate the exact content they want. Your role as the user is to help the AI help you! You want to provide directions that are as clear and unambiguous as possible so that the AI does not have to guess what you are thinking.

Once you are able to guide the AI, it will help you ensure that you get more relevant and coherent responses. It will also prevent frustration from spending a lot of time on trial-and-error and streamline the use of AI in your workflow. Once you know what kinds of prompts work best for the type of output you want, you can tailor them to your particular needs and customize them further.

Features of Effective Prompts

Prompts that work best have the following characteristics:

Clarity: Write clear and concise prompts, ensuring the AI can understand the intended task or question. Avoid using ambiguous words or language, and do not add unnecessary information.

Specificity: Be specific about the AI-generated response's desired format, context, or content. Refrain from making it guess about anything that you already know you want from it or that it should consider.

Open-endedness: Encourage creativity and exploration by leaving room for interpretation while providing sufficient guidance. If you are open to creativity or looking for ideas, use more open-ended questions or instructions regarding the desired output.

Scaffolding: Provide background information, examples, or constraints when necessary to help the AI generate more accurate and relevant content. Think about how much detail and direction you have to provide students to get them to do a task properly, and offer more than that!

Iteration: Be prepared to refine and adjust prompts based on AI-generated output, continuously improving the effectiveness of the prompt. If something doesn't work, think about what else you can say initially to get it right in one go.

Chain-prompting: If you have a complex task, you can scaffold it and feed it to the AI in steps rather than all at once. This way, you can ensure the output is correct at each stage before moving on to the next phase of the process. You can also use it to generate more extended outputs by having it create small pieces one at a time.

Examples of prompts that meet these criteria will be shared in future chapters, and a prompt database with tried and tested prompts for teachers is available on our website at pedagog.ai. We have included a variety of prompt styles, so you can try and test what works best for you and the AI tool you choose.

Getting Better at Prompt Writing

Prompt writing is a skill like any other, and while AI systems can make many more interpretations than previously thought possible, effective use will still require users to be intentional about their prompts. For example, in order to become a better "prompter," you can do the following:

- **Practice:** Regularly write and experiment with different types of prompts to build proficiency and experience. Try out different suggestions and see what works best.

- **Analyze AI responses:** Carefully examine AI-generated content to identify areas for improvement in prompt writing.

- **Collaborate:** Share and discuss prompts with colleagues, gaining insights and feedback to enhance prompt-writing abilities.

- **Learn from AI guidelines:** Study guidelines and best practices AI developers provide to understand the nuances of effective prompt writing.

- **Seek professional development:** Participate in workshops, webinars, or courses focusing on AI in education and prompt writing.

Once you find prompts that work for you, create a personal database of them so you can use them in the future. You should also experiment with the same prompts in different tools to see if they work better or produce different outcomes for you! Here are some general categories for collecting your own prompts:

- **Personalized learning:** Design prompts that address individual students' needs, learning styles, or interests.

- **Diverse perspectives:** Craft prompts that encourage AI-generated content to present multiple viewpoints or solutions.

- **Formative assessment:** Create prompts that generate quizzes, questions, or tasks that align with learning objectives.

- **Creative exploration:** Write prompts that students can use to inspire them to explore new topics, study concepts, or strengthen their knowledge base.

- **Support and scaffolding:** Draft prompts that generate instructional materials, examples, or explanations that help students better understand complex concepts or tasks.

CONCLUSION

As we conclude Chapter 2, it is important to remember that understanding the basics of AI and its applications in education is essential for educators to harness the full potential of AI in the classroom. By grasping the underlying concepts, principles, and methods of AI, teachers can make informed decisions regarding using and integrating AI tools in their teaching practices.

Throughout this chapter, we have introduced the main concepts and terminology in AI, explored the different types of machine learning, and discussed the implications of generative AI in education. We have also emphasized the importance of effective prompt writing and provided guidance on how teachers can improve their skills in this area.

As AI evolves and becomes more integrated into education, educators must stay informed about the latest developments and best practices. Therefore, the subsequent chapters of this book delve deeper into various aspects of AI in education, including ethics, assessment, personalization, and more. By equipping themselves with this knowledge, educators will be better prepared to navigate the complex landscape of AI-driven education and empower their students to thrive in the future.

Exit Ticket

Create an account on one of the popular generative AI tools (e.g., ChatGPT, Bard, Bing Chat, or Claude) if you haven't already, and begin by asking it to do a task you have on your to-do list. Then, see if you can refine your prompt to get your desired output.

Chapter 3

Reframing Education in the Age of AI

The age of AI will dramatically overhaul the workforce. By some accounts, AI will create more jobs than it destroys, but these jobs will require different skills and education levels than the ones displaced by automation. For example, AI may increase the demand for data scientists, software engineers, and machine learning specialists while reducing the need for clerks, cashiers, and drivers. More generally, AI will transform the nature of work and the skills required for workers, creating opportunities and challenges for employers and employees. For instance, AI may enhance human performance by providing better decision support, feedback, and training, but it may also pose ethical, legal, and social issues related to privacy, accountability, and bias.

Governments may provide universal basic incomes in response to a reduction in the labor market. The educational threshold for entering the workforce may increase such that more and more individuals need to be more advanced than the AI systems we are building.

We do not fully know the ramifications of AI, and it is not the job of this book to try to predict them, but we can safely say that the world will be very different.

This all means that the world we are preparing our students to enter after graduation is not the same world that will exist when they step outside the doors of their schools. And, of course, preparing students for the workforce is not the only purpose of education, but the other angles don't look too promising if we maintain the status quo in education. What it means to participate in democratic discussion and civic action will likely look different, as well as what it means to live a fulfilling and engaging life. The dramatic overhaul of our society's foundations means that we will likely have to shift our educational philosophies and practices in response to the growth of AI.

This chapter outlines how we can reframe the purpose of education and, thus, our practices to ensure that students are prepared for whatever the world looks like as the age of AI develops. While it may seem daunting to think about such a different society, you'll notice that the underlying principles and values that motivate our educational systems are fundamentally the same.

To prepare students for an AI-driven workforce, we'll have to shift the focus from creating "generators," which was the primary goal in the age of information, to creating "evaluators." It is very likely that for the foreseeable future, we will still rely on experts in various domains to tell us if the outputs generated by AI systems are accurate and effective. For example, a curriculum written by an AI system will likely be evaluated by education and domain knowledge experts. We will thus have to make sure our students are better equipped to become experts in their fields who have the reasoning and critical thinking skills to properly evaluate and apply the output generated by AI systems. We will also likely continue to value human connection and relationships, and students with the socioemotional skills to navigate that territory will likely fare better than those without.

We must ensure our students can safely and effectively navigate and use AI systems. They will need the skills to know how to use AI, recognize its shortcomings, and identify where it will need human augmentation. We must also ensure students have computational thinking skills to design products, services, and systems that build on AI systems. We'll need to make interdisciplinary connections between AI and various disciplines early on to achieve these goals effectively. AI cannot remain a topic only covered in computer science classrooms, but must be integrated across our curriculum to ensure students are prepared to apply AI skills and literacy in various fields.

Just like we will need to gain the skills to keep learning and growing in our practice as educators, students will need the right growth mindset and learning skills to continue to adapt to a changing world. They will need to rapidly pick up a new skill set, learn about new technology, and reapply their foundational skills and knowledge to new domains. They will have to do all this without becoming discouraged or disheartened when an AI system replaces them.

Finally, we must encourage students to think creatively and innovate to further human progress. They should be able to take advantage of the opportunities created by AI systems that take over routine and mundane tasks. AI can allow more individuals to take on creative and innovative roles as the repetitive and tedious tasks are taken over by machines.

PREPARING STUDENTS FOR THE AI-DRIVEN WORKFORCE

- How is AI changing the job market?
- What skills are essential for success in the AI-driven workforce?
- How can educators help students develop these skills?

If you've walked into a grocery store in the last few years, you've probably noticed the automated checkout lanes increase in frequency. With fewer humans at the checkout process and more automated processes, the grocery store can hire fewer employees than ever before. These changes are not unique to grocery stores and will likely spread beyond supermarkets within the next few years. As AI and robotics continue to improve, the jobs remaining on the market will continue to shift, and many jobs will likely become obsolete, forcing workers to reskill. The arrival of generative AI has increased the tasks AI can do and increased the number of jobs that a machine, rather than a human, will soon perform.

Here are a few key job markets that will change:

- **Retail:** Self-checkout kiosks and online shopping are reducing the need for human cashiers and salespeople.

- **Transportation:** Self-driving cars and trucks are being developed that could eventually replace human drivers.

- **Manufacturing:** Robots are being used to automate many tasks in manufacturing, such as welding, painting, and assembly; as these become connected to more advanced AI systems, they will be able to further reduce the need for human intervention and quality control.

- **Data entry:** AI-powered tools can automate many tasks performed by data entry clerks, such as extracting data from documents and entering it into databases.

- **Customer service:** AI-powered chatbots will answer customer questions and resolve issues. AI services, like Intercom, can already use company documentation and information to answer questions.

- **Copywriting:** AI-powered writing tools can edit, draft, and publish content, from press releases and social media posts to news articles and white papers.

- **Accounting:** AI-powered software can automate many tasks currently performed by accountants, such as preparing financial statements and auditing financial records. They can help categorize information and transactions and help explain financial statements.

- **Legal:** AI-powered tools can automate many tasks currently performed by lawyers, such as legal research and document review. They could prepare drafts of legal documents, file paperwork, and review work before it is submitted.

- **Medical:** AI-powered tools can diagnose diseases, recommend treatments, and perform surgery. They can also interface directly with patients to gather basic information, collect medical history, and explain results and diagnoses, even in multiple languages.

- **Financial:** AI-powered tools can be used to make investment decisions, manage risk, and detect fraud. For example, they can sift through millions of articles, emails, and calls and understand the sentiment around a particular company to inform investment decisions.

While these are just a few jobs that will likely be replaced or look very different in the near future, there are many more examples as different industries and companies explore applications of AI and robotics in their daily practice. In general, it is likely already possible that most work that can be repetitive or synthesis-based (using a lot of information to make decisions or judgments) can be replaced by AI.

As AI progresses and society becomes more comfortable and trusting of these technologies, the job market will shift to a heavier focus on other areas. Not all changes will be bad! New jobs are likely to be created in response to the boom (e.g., AI ethicists and AI trainers), and workers will be more productive as they rely on AI tools and can focus on growth and innovation. Here are a few examples of job markets that will likely see a boom:

- **Creative industries:** While AI can generate content, the human touch in creative fields like art, music, and writing is irreplaceable. The creative process often involves intuition, emotion, and a deep understanding of human experience, which are areas where AI still falls short. Also, human-generated creativity will likely be viewed as more "authentic" and thus more valuable.

- **Healthcare:** While AI can assist in diagnosis and treatment, human intuition and judgment in healthcare are crucial. Nurses, doctors, and other healthcare professionals who provide patient care will continue to be in high demand. Additionally, mental health professionals, such as psychologists and therapists, will continue to be needed.

- **Education:** AI can provide personalized learning experiences, but educators who can inspire, motivate, and understand the unique needs of their students will always be necessary. Teachers, professors, and other educators will continue to be essential.

- **Social services:** Jobs that involve helping people, such as social workers, counselors, and therapists, will continue to be necessary. These roles require empathy, understanding, and navigating complex human emotions and situations. They also involve trust and human relationships to reach the most vulnerable.

- **Research and development:** As technology advances, there will be a growing need for professionals who can develop, implement, and manage these new technologies. This includes AI specialists, data scientists, and engineers. Most STEM markets will increase in size and begin to centralize around AI-based technology.

While there are likely to be new job markets created as we find new ways to spend our time and talent, these existing industries will see an increased need for more workers.

Students will need to develop the right skills to succeed in these markets and grow their careers as the job market continues to evolve with the increase in AI capabilities. The AI-driven workforce will require a mix of technical and soft skills. Here are a few critical skills that will be essential:

- **Technical skills:** At least a basic understanding of AI and machine learning concepts, programming languages, data analysis, and cybersecurity will be crucial no matter which industry students enter.

- **Problem-solving:** As AI takes over repetitive tasks, human workers will be needed to tackle complex problems that require critical thinking and innovative solutions.

- **Creativity:** The ability to think creatively and develop innovative ideas will be highly valued. Being able to make aesthetic judgments, come up with radically new ideas and designs, and respond to human needs will set apart creatives who solely rely on AI to produce versus creatives who use AI as a tool.

- **Emotional intelligence:** The ability to understand and navigate human emotions will be crucial, especially in fields like education, healthcare, and social services.

- **Lifelong learning:** Continuous learning and adapting will be essential as technology evolves. *The most important skill students need to learn is how to keep learning.*

Teachers can foster these skills in students by shifting their focus in the classroom to more open-ended and creative activities while ensuring that students acquire the foundational skills necessary to navigate existing and new markets. Certain strategies already employed in classrooms will become more critical:

- **Developing Critical Thinking and Problem-Solving Skills**
  - Using project-based learning to provide hands-on, real-world experiences that challenge students to think critically, collaborate, and innovate.
  - Encouraging students to analyze complex situations, synthesize information, and make informed decisions.

- **Promoting Collaboration Skills**
  - Creating learning environments that motivate students to work together, share ideas, and learn from one another.
  - Enhancing communication and collaboration skills, encouraging students to work effectively with diverse teams, and leveraging collective intelligence.
  - Stimulating students to explore connections between subjects, fostering creative problem-solving and adaptability.

- **Fostering Adaptability**
  - Acknowledging that the pace of change is accelerating, students must be able to adapt to new technologies and ways of working.
  - Motivating students to view challenges as opportunities for growth, helping them develop resilience and a mentality for lifelong learning.
  - Prioritizing the development of transferable skills over specific content knowledge to prepare students for various industries and job roles.

- **Enhancing Digital Literacy**
  - Integrating AI and digital tools into the curriculum equips students with the necessary skills and knowledge to succeed in an AI-driven workforce.
  - Teaching students to effectively use, navigate, and understand digital tools and technologies, including AI systems.
  - Recognizing that AI is powered by data, thus, students need to effectively collect, analyze, and interpret data.
- **Boosting Socioemotional Intelligence**
  - Fostering an understanding of one's emotions encourages students to manage their feelings effectively.
  - Encouraging empathy toward others is a skill that remains uniquely human.
  - Facilitating the ability to learn from experience, embrace change, and navigate uncertainty in a rapidly evolving workforce.

The rest of this chapter and most of the following provide concrete steps and ideas to help shift classrooms toward these focuses as we prepare students to enter an AI-dominant job market.

DEVELOPING AI LITERACY AND COMPUTATIONAL THINKING

- What is AI literacy, and why is it important for students?
- What are the core concepts and skills required for AI literacy?
- How can schools incorporate AI literacy into the curriculum?

As AI continues to permeate our society, students must comprehensively understand this technology to critically evaluate its implications. Understanding AI's functionality and thinking critically about its consequences are essential skills students will require in the age of AI. By fostering this understanding, we can equip them with the necessary tools to navigate an increasingly digital world, encompassing their personal and professional spheres. Empowered with the right knowledge and skills, students can make informed decisions about the ethical, social, and technological implications of AI use, considering potential biases, privacy issues, and ethical implications. As highlighted in the preceding section, the rapid job market shift also necessitates students' active participation in the rapidly evolving, AI-driven job landscape. Adapting to more of these future changes will be crucial, making fostering foundational AI literacy and comfort in schools an indispensable first step.

The core concepts and skills required for AI literacy include being able to answer the following questions:

- What are AI and machine learning, and what tools already exist?
- Why is AI a significant development for society?
- Where will I encounter AI in my personal and professional life?
- How can I use AI to solve my problems?
- When might I choose to use or not use AI or a particular tool?

This book aims to foster AI literacy for teachers by making sure you can answer those questions for yourself by the end of reading it. Similarly, students should be able to answer those questions for themselves when they leave our schools. To be able to answer these questions effectively, schools will have to ensure that there is a focus on:

- **Fundamentals of AI:** Grasping AI's fundamental concepts and principles, machine learning, and related technologies.
- **Data literacy:** The ability to interpret, analyze, and evaluate data, understanding its role in AI-driven decision-making processes.

- **Computational thinking:** The ability to logically break down complex problems into smaller, manageable steps, a crucial skill for understanding AI algorithms.

- **Critical thinking and evaluation:** Developing the ability to critically assess AI systems' and applications' strengths, limitations, and potential biases.

- **Ethical awareness:** Understanding the ethical implications and social consequences of AI use, such as privacy concerns, fairness, and accountability.

- **Digital citizenship:** Developing responsible and safe online behavior as well as an awareness of the impact of AI on society and individuals.

To ensure that students fully develop these skills, we must do more than teach them what AI is in a standalone computer science class. We will have to incorporate the following into our classrooms:

- **Interdisciplinary integration:** Embed AI concepts and skills across various subjects, illustrating their relevance and applicability in diverse contexts.

- **Project-based learning:** Assign projects that challenge students to apply their understanding of AI concepts and principles.

- **AI-driven tools and platforms:** Utilize AI-driven educational tools, such as adaptive learning platforms and intelligent tutoring systems, to expose students to AI technologies in practice.

- **Ethical discussions and case studies:** Encourage critical thinking and ethical reflection by exploring AI-related case studies, dilemmas, and scenarios.

Integrating AI literacy into traditional subject areas will ensure that students can adapt what they are learning in any context they find themselves in. For example, in math, students can learn about AI by exploring how algorithms solve problems and how machine learning works. In science, students can learn about AI by exploring how AI is used to make medical diagnoses or to develop new drugs. In social studies, students can learn about AI by exploring how AI is used to make decisions about things like criminal justice or immigration. Other examples of cross-curricular uses of AI include:

- **AI and art:** Students can explore AI-generated art or use AI tools to create artwork, examining the intersection of creativity, technology, and culture.

- **AI and data visualization:** Students can create data-driven visualizations using AI tools, exploring the relationship among data, design, and storytelling.

- **AI and environmental science:** Students can use AI to analyze and predict environmental changes, examining the potential for AI-driven solutions in addressing climate change and other global challenges.

- **AI and robotics:** Students can design and build AI-powered robots, exploring the integration of engineering, programming, and AI to solve real-world problems.

- **AI and ethics:** Students can engage in debates and discussions around the ethical implications of AI applications in different fields, such as healthcare, criminal justice, and environmental conservation.

Sample lesson plans with ideas for integration can be found at pedagog.ai.

As you learn how to incorporate AI-based tools into your practice, take some time to think about how you will share with students how AI plays a role in your career. Also, think about how you can directly expose students to AI in your assignments and projects to help develop these AI literacy skills through practice. Chapters 7 and 8 focus on more practical examples across disciplines.

FOSTERING A GROWTH MINDSET AND LIFELONG LEARNING CULTURE

- How does a growth mindset impact students' success in the AI-driven world?
- What role do educators play in fostering a lifelong learning culture?
- How can AI enhance self-directed learning?

One of the key implications of AI on our society is the rapid pace at which change will continue to take place. In the next few decades, AI will likely profoundly impact every aspect of society, from how we work to how we interact with each other. As covered in the first section, the most dramatic change will be in the job market, and the kinds of work humans still need to do. We also discussed the emergence of new fields, more time for creativity and innovation, and other implications of offloading a lot of work to AI systems and creating more space for human flourishing.

In the past, technological change has typically been gradual and incremental, and we've had plenty of time to adapt to it. However, AI is changing the world at an exponential rate. This means that it is difficult to predict what the future holds. However, AI will significantly impact every part of society, and it is important to start thinking about how we can prepare for this change.

Students will need resilience and a growth mindset to overcome the kinds of challenges that such rapid shifts create. They need to see these changes as opportunities to frame the dynamic nature of the future workforce as an opportunity to grow and flourish rather than find themselves behind or obsolete. A vital component of that growth mindset will likely come from developing a habit of continuous learning, with a strong sense of curiosity and a desire to stay relevant through the pursuit of knowledge.

Students must also see themselves as problem-solvers to approach complex problems that AI cannot solve with creativity and persistence. They will need to both have the self-confidence that they can take ownership of their lifelong learning journey and a collaborative mindset so that they seek feedback and learn from others.

As AI continues to automate many hard skills, soft skills such as communication, leadership, empathy, and adaptability will become increasingly important. These skills, which are more challenging for AI to replicate, require a growth mindset emphasizing continuous learning and development. They are also opportunities for lifelong growth and learning as students continue to develop their soft skills and learn to apply them to various situations.

Educators will have to role model these dispositions themselves. By committing to keeping up with the latest developments and incorporating them into your practice, you are already helping to set an example of the need to adapt and maintain curiosity for students.

The projects and assignments in our classrooms will also have to make sure they encourage curiosity, exploration, and inquiry rather than focus on any particular piece of knowledge or a single skill. Our school reward systems and rhetoric also need to continue to emphasize students' effort and progress rather than solely performance to foster a growth-oriented mentality.

AI tools will help make some of these tasks more manageable by providing educators with the options to personalize and adapt to each student's learning journey. The more students see their learning journeys as long-term and personal, the more likely they are to be able to build the habits needed to continue those outside the classroom walls. AI-powered tools can provide learning adapted to each student's learning style and needs, provide them instant feedback and recommendations based on their performance, suggest resources and further learning paths, and help them develop the skill set to use AI to guide and aid their learning throughout their lives. As AI bots become more prevalent in classrooms, helping frame them as a permanent part of the students' lives will be crucial to building a lifelong learning mindset.

As we think about how we adapt our pedagogical practices in Chapter 4, you will see that most mainstream pedagogical theories support building these kinds of dispositions in students, and the ability to reframe and connect these to the age of AI will be much easier than it may seem.

CULTIVATING CREATIVITY AND INNOVATION SKILLS IN THE AI ERA

- What are the benefits of cultivating creativity and innovation skills in the AI era?

- How can educators encourage students to be innovative thinkers?

- How can AI foster creativity and innovation in the classroom?

- How can interdisciplinary learning encourage innovation?

As we navigate the era of AI, our roles as educators become increasingly pivotal in fostering creativity and innovation within our students. AI promises to automate numerous tasks traditionally carried out by humans, freeing up our intellectual capacities to direct more focus toward pioneering innovation. Moreover, AI's potential to generate ideas and solutions beyond human imagination underscores the importance of developing these capabilities within our students. Our students will need the ability to put into practice those ideas, challenge them, and iterate on the ideas generated by AI.

By fostering these skills, we equip our students for a rapidly evolving future and also empower our students to contribute toward human progress by equipping them to identify opportunities and create value in the AI era.

Outside of the job market, as more time is freed up for personal development and pursuits by automated tasks, students will need the ability to exercise their own creativity in meaningful ways to live engaging, flourishing lives. Developing a habit of thinking outside the box will help students find new ways to build meaning and purpose in their own lives through increased self-expression and personal growth.

Educators need to create an environment that encourages students to be innovative thinkers. We can provide a supportive classroom space that encourages risk-taking, experimentation, and learning from failures. Emphasizing growth and development over performance will help students feel empowered to try things without risking repercussions. Incorporating activities that promote teamwork and collaboration will help them learn to share ideas and build upon each other's perspectives. Providing students with more agency in what projects they do and how they signal mastery of a concept will help students have the space to apply knowledge in creative ways. While these are all things most teachers already aspire to, finding more ways to center these goals rather than use them as a means to content-area mastery will help teachers and students reframe the purpose and aim of these activities in the age of AI.

Educators can also use AI itself to help foster a creative mindset and help students develop the habit of using technology as a resource during their creative process. Some examples of creative projects teachers can assign students include:

- **AI-generated art:** Students can explore AI-generated art or create their own using AI-powered tools like DeepArt.io or RunwayML.

- **AI-assisted music composition:** Students can use AI tools, like AIVA or Amper Music, to compose music or analyze the structure of existing pieces.

- **AI-powered storytelling:** Students can experiment with AI-powered language models like ChatGPT to generate creative writing pieces or analyze narrative structures.

- **AI-enhanced graphic design:** Students can use AI-driven design platforms like Adobe Sensei to create and edit visual projects.

- **AI in fashion:** Students can investigate AI applications like virtual try-on experiences or AI-generated clothing designs.

- **AI-assisted game design:** Students can explore game development using AI tools to generate levels, characters, or other game elements.

A key component for cultivating innovative and creative skills in our students will be a shift away from the compartmentalized structure of our current school systems. The future will be sculpted by those capable of thinking outside the boxes of traditional disciplines, and as educators, we need to instill this mindset in our classrooms. Encouraging our students to build connections across different disciplines increases their ability to think innovatively in their personal and future professional lives.

Interdisciplinary learning helps students visualize the larger picture, explore different perspectives, and comprehend the interconnectedness of our world. Shifting toward more interdisciplinary curricula will give our students the skills to navigate and make meaningful contributions in a world shaped by AI. By learning to draw connections between different disciplines, students can develop the ability to approach complex, real-world challenges from a variety of angles. Interdisciplinary learning also promotes adaptability and helps students become agile thinkers who can adjust to new contexts and situations. The broader perspective will also help students develop an appreciation for the global (both metaphorically and literally) implications of their actions and decisions.

AI itself can be used to help foster interdisciplinary thinking! Some projects that would allow students to use multiple different skill sets and knowledge bases include:

- **Data analysis:** AI tools can help students analyze and interpret complex data sets, fostering critical thinking and data literacy across disciplines.

- **Exploration of bias:** AI-driven discussions on algorithmic bias and fairness can promote critical thinking about the implications of AI in various domains.

- **Real-world problem-solving:** AI tools can simulate real-world scenarios, challenging students to apply critical thinking skills to solve interdisciplinary problems.

- **Enhancing creativity:** AI-powered creative tools can inspire students to think critically about the role of technology in art, design, and other creative disciplines.

- **AI and research:** AI tools can aid students in identifying, evaluating, and synthesizing information from diverse sources, promoting critical thinking in research and inquiry.

In later chapters of this book, as we explain how you can use AI tools to do this and more, you'll start to see how easy developing creativity and innovation will be with AI tools at our disposal.

CONCLUSION

As we advance into the age of AI, the landscape of our society, and consequently education, will undergo a significant transformation.

While it may appear daunting, it is clear that we need to reframe the purpose of education and our practices to keep pace with the rise of AI and prepare our students for the world they will soon inhabit.

Our students must be capable of becoming evaluators, with sharp reasoning and critical thinking skills, ready to criticize and use the outputs of AI systems. We must encourage their socioemotional capabilities to navigate an environment rich in human connection and relationships, despite the prevalence of machines. Importantly, we must equip our students with the knowledge and skills to utilize AI systems, understand their limitations, and build on them where necessary.

Computational thinking will be a vital skill, allowing students to design products and systems that build on AI and understand systems that others build. We need to ensure AI literacy across various disciplines, not confine it to the realm of computer science, and break down the barriers within disciplines to model the complexity of the real world. Students must be ready to adapt, learn, and apply their foundational knowledge to new domains, showing resilience when faced with the prospect of AI systems replacing them. In addition, we must foster creativity and innovation in our students, enabling them to capitalize on the opportunities provided by AI and push the boundaries of human progress.

Our educational systems' fundamental principles and values remain the same, even though the context and learning tools are changing rapidly. The primary goal of education, to prepare students for life beyond the classroom, remains unaltered. However, the "life" they will enter will be markedly different. This responsibility may be immense, but it is a challenge we must meet. As educators, our task is to ensure that today's students are ready to become the leaders, innovators, and citizens of the AI-driven world of tomorrow.

Exit Ticket

Go through your curricular goals for the year. Try to see how many will be relevant in the age of AI. What would you change or add? If you can't control the content you must teach, how can you incorporate the skills discussed in this chapter into your teaching practice?

Chapter 4

Adapting Pedagogy for AI Integration

The prevailing alarmist sentiment often suggests that our entire educational system has become, or is becoming, outdated. Despite this, modern pedagogical theory, informed by centuries of educational research and practice, is resilient and robust enough to adapt and evolve, even in the face of perhaps the most remarkable shift since John Dewey began his influential writings. Therefore, rather than resisting this change, we have begun to reframe our perspective, as is discussed in Chapter 3, to modify our pedagogical theories and practices in the era of AI. In many instances, AI can enhance our existing practices, thereby facilitating us in achieving our educational goals more effectively.

Adapting our educational practice to accommodate the changes brought about by AI will empower us to fully harness the potential of AI in improving learning outcomes and experiences. Despite advancements in our current practices, such as incorporating social-emotional learning (SEL), leveraging digital tools, and shifting toward mastery learning, we continue to grapple with the challenge of student engagement. AI presents an opportunity to address the root causes of many of the problems we face in education. With the capacity to personalize and enhance interactivity and immersion in learning experiences, AI can improve the efficiency and effectiveness of instruction while better supporting individual student needs.

In the upcoming sections, we delve deeper into the intersection of AI and pedagogy. We will explore a range of learning theories — including constructivist, behaviorist, and sociocultural approaches — and how they evolve in the AI era. Finally, we discuss how AI can transform active classroom learning, enhancing student engagement and motivation.

We also examine how problem- and project-based learning strategies can be supercharged with AI tools, fostering a more collaborative and dynamic learning environment. The section on Bloom's Taxonomy considers how critical thinking skills can be developed in an AI-enhanced classroom, while the part on differentiated instruction demonstrates how AI can generate customized activities to cater to the diverse learning needs of students.

Furthermore, we discuss how AI integration can foster collaboration and relationship-building among students and how it can support inquiry-based learning, encouraging student-centered exploration. Throughout, we highlight the potential of AI not just as a tool, but also as a catalyst for a paradigm shift in education.

It is crucial to understand that adapting our pedagogy to include AI should be viewed as a symbiotic integration, not a replacement. We stand at the precipice of a new era in education, and it is through this blending of traditional pedagogical strategies with innovative AI technologies that we can usher in this new age of learning.

LEARNING THEORIES IN THE AI ERA: CONSTRUCTIVIST, BEHAVIORIST, AND SOCIOCULTURAL APPROACHES

- What role does AI play in knowledge construction?
- How can AI support reinforcement and feedback in behaviorist approaches?
- How does AI enhance collaboration and cultural diversity in sociocultural approaches?

As we enter the age of AI, we will have to intertwine AI with the three primary learning theories: constructivist, behaviorist, and sociocultural. We can enhance these approaches by using AI-powered tools and AI-built resources to facilitate more efficient and effective learning experiences for our students. This chapter not only provides a theoretical exploration of these topics, but also offers practical advice and suggestions for educators to effectively integrate these approaches into their classrooms. We explore how AI can be harnessed to augment traditional pedagogical methods and create an environment responsive to every learner's needs. These ideas also serve as the starting point for later sections and chapters that delve further into particular practices that fit within these theories.

AI and the Constructivist Approach

The constructivist theory of learning posits that learners actively construct their own understanding and knowledge of the world through experiences and reflection. In the AI era, the knowledge construction process will be reshaped. AI can act as a catalyst for active learning, scaffolding students, personalizing learning trajectories, and fostering a deeper understanding. Here are some general ways AI will help with knowledge construction:

- **Facilitating inquiry:** AI tools can provide students access to vast resources and information, enabling them to explore and investigate topics independently. For example, students can use Perplexity.ai, ChatGPT, Bard, and Bing Chat to start the inquiry process and determine which learning path to pursue.

- **Personalized learning:** AI-driven platforms can adapt to individual learners' needs and interests, helping students construct knowledge at their own pace and level of understanding. AI tools can help students identify what they might be interested in, what they need to learn to pursue a particular learning path, and what they need to reinforce to ensure they are learning effectively. Tools like Socrat.ai, Quizlet's Q-Chat, and Khanmigo can serve as students' personal learning guides.

- **Problem-solving:** AI-powered simulations and virtual environments can engage students in authentic problem-solving activities, promoting the construction of knowledge through experience. Teachers can also use AI to generate simulations to use in their classrooms.

- **Scaffolding:** AI technologies can provide customized scaffolding and support, helping students progressively construct their understanding and bridge gaps in knowledge. Teachers can either generate the scaffolding, or students can seek it themselves.

- **Knowledge visualization:** AI tools can help students visualize and organize complex information, assisting them in constructing connections and deeper understanding. Teachers can present information in various ways, and students can seek different representations independently.

- **Reflection and metacognition:** AI-driven questioning can support students in reflecting on their learning process, fostering metacognitive skills, and promoting knowledge construction.

AI can help students craft their understanding of the world through a personalized discovery and exploration process that allows them to experience knowledge in the ways most valuable to them and reflect on their learning process.

Prompt It!

- **Discovery Learning:** "Generate a hypothetical archaeological site report. Ask the students to interpret the data and draw conclusions about the civilization that might have lived there."

- **Problem-Based Learning:** "Describe a real-world environmental issue and ask students to brainstorm and propose their own solutions using the scientific method."

- **Inquiry-Based Learning:** "Create a scenario about a mysterious historical event. Provide students with primary source documents to analyze and construct their own interpretation of the event."

- **Reflective Learning:** "Create an essay prompt for students to write a reflective essay on their personal growth throughout the school year, highlighting key events, changes, and areas of improvement."

- **Concept Mapping:** "Present a complex topic, such as the human circulatory system, and ask students to create a concept map showing how the different elements are interconnected. Provide a starting point for them with a partial map."

- **Cognitive Flexibility:** "Present a complex scientific phenomenon, such as climate change, from various scientific disciplines' perspectives. Ask students to integrate this information and form their own comprehensive understanding."

- **Experiential Learning:** "Describe a hypothetical field trip to a local business. Ask students to consider the roles of different employees, the business model, and how they would apply what they learned in their future careers."

AI and the Behaviorist Approach

The behaviorist theory emphasizes learning as a response to environmental stimuli and posits that behaviors can be shaped through reinforcement and feedback. AI can provide real-time, personalized feedback and reinforcement, enhancing the efficiency of learning and paving the way for behaviorist approaches to be implemented at scale. Here are some ways that AI can be used for reinforcement and feedback:

- **Immediate feedback:** AI-powered platforms can provide real-time, personalized student performance feedback, reinforcing positive behaviors and correcting misconceptions.

- **Adaptive learning:** AI-driven learning systems can tailor content and practice activities to individual learners' needs, reinforcing desired behaviors and skills.

- **Gamification:** AI technologies can incorporate gamification elements, such as rewards and badges, to motivate and reinforce students' learning and engagement.

- **Progress monitoring:** AI tools can track students' progress and performance, allowing educators to provide targeted reinforcement and feedback.

- **Mastery-based learning:** AI systems can support mastery-based learning approaches, ensuring that students understand concepts deeply before progressing to more advanced material.

- **Data-driven insights:** AI-generated analytics can help educators identify patterns and trends in student performance, informing targeted reinforcement strategies.

While most of the behaviorist approaches will require technologists to build applications that utilize the power of AI, there are some quick ways that you can start using AI on your own through the following suggested prompts.

Prompt It!

- **Reinforcement Learning:** "Create a series of long-division multiple-choice problems, each with difficulty scores out of 5, numbered 1–30. The worksheet should indicate that they should do the question in each difficulty tier until they get two right, and then move on to the next tier."

- **Drill and Practice:** "Generate a list of 50 vocabulary words and their respective definitions for an English as a Second Language (ESL) class. Then, create a drill practice with a series of sentences where students have to fill in the blanks with the appropriate words."

- **Spaced Repetition:** "Design a schedule for reviewing Spanish vocabulary words, using the principles of spaced repetition to enhance memory retention."

- **Mastery Learning:** "Draft a sequence of lessons on quadratic equations, where students must demonstrate mastery of each subtopic before moving on to the next."

- **Shaping:** "Develop a series of lessons that gradually teach students how to write a persuasive essay, starting with the basics of argument structure and gradually introducing more complex elements."

- **Stimulus-Response Learning:** "Generate a series of 'If . . . then . . .' scenarios to teach students about cause-and-effect in ecosystems."

AI and the Sociocultural Approach

Finally, the sociocultural theory emphasizes that learning happens within social contexts and is profoundly influenced by cultural beliefs and attitudes. AI can support the facilitation of global classrooms, enable collaborative learning experiences that transcend geographical boundaries, and help learners appreciate and understand various cultural perspectives. Here are some ways that AI can help adapt to cultural and social contexts:

- **Global connections:** AI-driven platforms can connect students with peers and experts from diverse cultural backgrounds, fostering collaboration and the co-construction of knowledge. For example, platforms might automatically pair students with similar interests, translate text into each student's target language, and provide prompts during conversations to guide the conversation constructively.

- **Language translation:** AI-powered translation tools can break down language barriers, enabling seamless communication and collaboration among learners from different linguistic backgrounds.

- **Cultural insights:** AI technologies can provide students access to diverse cultural perspectives and resources, enriching their understanding and appreciation of different worldviews. For example, AI tools can rewrite the same story from the perspective of different cultures and allow students to analyze the differences.

- **Project-based learning:** AI technologies can support interdisciplinary, project-based learning experiences that encourage collaboration and the integration of diverse perspectives by helping teachers craft unique projects based on curricular goals.

- **Inclusive design:** AI-driven adaptive systems can ensure that learning experiences are accessible and inclusive for learners with diverse needs, backgrounds, and abilities, supporting a sociocultural approach to education. More on this is discussed in the following section on differentiation.

The ability of generative AI to quickly rewrite content, create scenarios and dialogues, and understand the sentiment and content of conversations increases the potential for the use of AI in sociocultural classrooms.

Prompt It!

- **Collaborative Learning:** "Design a complex task, such as building a model of a sustainable city. Ask students to divide the roles among themselves and work together to complete the project."

- **Cultural Understanding:** "Generate a brief overview of different cultural celebrations worldwide. Ask students to research a chosen celebration and present their findings to the class."

- **Social Negotiation:** "Present a contentious historical event from multiple perspectives. Ask students to debate the event, considering these different viewpoints."

- **Role-playing:** "Create a scenario where students have to role-play as delegates from different countries during a United Nations conference on climate change. The goal is to reach an agreement that satisfies as many countries as possible."

- **Contextual Learning:** "Generate a task where students research and present how geographical and cultural factors influence the local cuisine in different regions of France."

- **Peer Teaching:** "Create an activity where students become 'experts' on different aspects of Roman history and then teach these topics to their peers."

- **Multi-Modal Learning:** "Create a project where students must present a historical event using various modes of expression: written report, oral presentation, and a visual (poster, slide show, etc.)."

- **Zone of Proximal Development:** "Design a series of increasingly challenging math problems where students start with problems they can solve independently and then gradually move onto problems that require peer or teacher assistance."

- **Cultural Responsiveness:** "Create an assignment where students research and present the impact of colonialism on different indigenous cultures around the world and how these cultures continue to resist and retain their identities."

ACTIVE LEARNING AND AI: TRANSFORMING THE CLASSROOM EXPERIENCE

- How can AI enrich active learning?
- How does AI bolster student autonomy and decision-making?
- How can AI support the development of metacognitive skills?

Active learning, which promotes student involvement and engagement, presents an opportunity for AI to contribute significantly. AI can enrich active learning, bolster student autonomy and decision-making, and foster the development of metacognitive skills in active learning environments.

In active learning classrooms, students are the key leaders in their education. They immerse themselves in the material and engage in discussions, group projects, and hands-on activities. The possible personalization with AI-powered systems helps cater learning to each student's individual goals. AI can customize lessons to cater to students' strengths, weaknesses, interests, and learning styles. This personalization allows each student to engage with the material in a way most beneficial to their learning journey.

AI can also expedite active learning by providing immediate feedback on assignments and quizzes. For example, an AI-powered quiz platform could highlight a student's recurring mistake in solving a specific type of math problem. This immediate feedback enables students to learn from errors and promptly modify their strategies.

AI can also support autonomy and decision-making by offering personalized recommendations based on a student's learning profile and progress. For example, imagine an AI system suggesting that a student who is a visual learner use a specific graphic-based resource to prepare for an upcoming biology test. AI can guide students in making more informed decisions by providing these personalized suggestions.

AI can also help foster metacognitive skills so that students are better equipped to make decisions about their own learning journeys. For example, AI can facilitate reflective activities, such as self-assessment quizzes or reflective journal prompts. An example might be an AI-driven journaling app that offers immediate, personalized feedback based on students' reflections, prompting them with further thoughtful questions based on their entries.

Prompt It!

- Teacher Prompts

  - **Discussion:** "Generate a step-by-step guide on how to conduct a successful group discussion on 'Climate Change' for a class of 9th graders."

  - **Gamify:** "Describe an interactive game that can be used to teach the concept of gravity to 5th graders."

  - **Student-Led Presentations:** "Design a lesson plan for an 8th-grade history class that incorporates student-led presentations."

  - **Active Learning Exercises:** "Develop a series of active learning exercises for a high school chemistry class on the topic of molecular structures."

  - **Suggestions:** "Suggest ways to incorporate technology into a 7th-grade math class to make learning more interactive and engaging."

  - **Self-Assessment:** "Explain how students can be allowed to assess their own performance in a science experiment in a 6th-grade class."

- **Student Choice:** "Design a lesson plan that integrates student choice into learning activities for a middle school geography class."

- **Self-Reflection:** "Describe a series of activities that can be used to help 7th-grade students improve their self-reflection skills in an English class."

- **Curricular Metacognition:** "Create a set of questions that a teacher can use to encourage metacognition during a discussion on 'The Industrial Revolution' in an 8th-grade history class."

- **Hands-On Learning:** "Outline a hands-on experiment for my physics class to demonstrate the principle of buoyancy."

- Student Prompts

  - **Topic Exploration:** "Help me brainstorm a list of potential topics for my research project in biology class."

  - **Self-Assessment:** "Guide me in creating a self-assessment rubric for my English essay assignment."

  - **Personalized Study Plan:** "Assist me in forming a study plan for my upcoming calculus exam based on my strengths and weaknesses."

  - **Research Buddy:** "Help me decide the most relevant sources to use for my history research paper."

  - **Prioritization Help:** "Provide me with strategies to prioritize tasks for my group project in geography class."

  - **Self-Reflection:** "Help me generate reflective questions to better understand my learning process in my Spanish class."

- **Scaffolding:** "Assist me in creating a checklist of steps to solve complex algebra problems."

- **Assessment Reflection:** "Guide me in analyzing my recent test performance to identify areas of improvement for my science class."

PROBLEM- AND PROJECT-BASED LEARNING STRATEGIES WITH AI

- Why are problem- and project-based learning even more important, given the developments in AI?

- How can AI be integrated into problem- and project-based learning activities?

- What are examples of project- and problem-based activities using AI?

As AI increasingly integrates into various industries, engaging students in problem- and project-based learning will prepare them for real-world applications of AI. Because problem- and project-based learning foster essential skills such as critical thinking, collaboration, communication, and creativity, they are crucial for success in an AI-driven workforce. Similarly, engaging students in complex, open-ended projects helps build adaptability and resilience — qualities we outlined as critical in an AI-driven world. Problem- and project-based learning also help foster the interdisciplinary thinking discussed in Chapter 3, encouraging students to draw on knowledge and skills from multiple disciplines to solve complex challenges. Finally, both learning approaches instill a growth mindset and promote lifelong learning through trial and error, and solution-based thinking.

One of the key challenges in both learning approaches is that they require a significant amount of preparation time from teachers, and the feedback and assessment might vary based on the path the students take. The introduction of AI tools should make both of these approaches easier to manage and implement. Some ways AI can be used for these strategies are:

- **Real-world simulations:** AI and virtual reality (VR) combined can make authentic simulations that help students role-play in a fully immersive and responsive environment. For example, they might be in a VR world where they campaign for office and have mock discussions with AI-powered constituents.

- **Data analysis and visualization:** AI tools can assist students in collecting, analyzing, and visualizing complex data sets during project-based learning experiences without becoming experts in statistical analysis. They can rely on AI systems to handle data while focusing on the implications and conclusions relevant to the curriculum.

- **Classroom activities:** AI can quickly develop scenarios, project ideas, rubrics, and assignments, which use one of the two approaches, for students without a significant investment of resources from educators.

- **Personalization:** AI can tailor project-based learning experiences to individual learners' needs and interests by adapting the projects depending on the information the student provides and customizing the components relevant to the curriculum.

- **Virtual mentors:** AI-driven chatbots and virtual assistants can provide students with guidance, support, and resources as they work on problem- and project-based learning activities, ensuring that students get the one-on-one support needed for complex assignments that might vary from student to student, which makes it harder for one classroom teacher to manage all the students.

- **Assessment and feedback:** Similarly, AI tools can generate real-time feedback and evaluation of students' work during problem- and project-based learning experiences and apply a standard rubric to different projects to help teachers quickly and accurately give feedback and assess students.

Not only can AI be used to streamline the project and problem-based activities, whether it be through existing generative AI chatbots or through future applications built using them, it can also directly inspire projects that require students to use AI themselves:

- **Social good:** In social studies, students could develop or plan AI-driven solutions to address local or global challenges, such as climate change, healthcare, or education equity.
- **Robotics and automation:** In robotics, students might design and build AI-powered robots to perform specific tasks or solve real-world problems, such as disaster response or environmental cleanup.
- **Natural language processing:** In language or health classes, students could create AI-driven chatbots or virtual assistants to provide information, support, or resources in various contexts, such as wellness support or language learning.
- **Art projects:** In art class, students might use AI tools to generate artwork, music, or other creative outputs that match curricular goals ("use AI to make a painting that Van Gogh might have painted if he still were around").
- **Ethics and bias:** In philosophy, sociology, or psychology classes, students might investigate the ethical implications of AI, exploring

issues such as algorithmic bias, data privacy, and the digital divide, and propose solutions to address these concerns.

Prompt It!

PROBLEM-BASED LEARNING

- Teacher Prompts

  - **Solution Assignment:** "Design a detailed assignment plan for a project where students must come up with potential solutions to the problem of plastic waste in our oceans. The assignment should include objectives, evaluation criteria, and a suggested timeline."

  - **Classroom Round Table:** "Generate a lesson plan for a class discussion on the ongoing energy crisis. The lesson should cover different perspectives, including renewable energy and traditional energy sources, and provide engaging activities for the students to understand these concepts."

  - **Background Material:** "Create a teaching resource pack to guide students in developing a step-by-step plan for a city aiming to reduce its carbon footprint within the next 10 years. The resource pack should include reference materials, worksheet templates, and potential discussion questions."

- Student Prompts

  - **Brainstorming:** "Generate a list of questions that a scientist might ask when trying to understand the impacts of climate change on polar ice caps."

- **Planning:** "Describe the steps I would need to take to start a community garden in an urban environment. What challenges might I face, and how could I overcome them?"

- **Researching:** "Help me understand the potential economic impact of introducing a new species into an ecosystem."

PROJECT-BASED LEARNING
- Teacher Prompts
  - **Scaffolding Projects:** "Provide a detailed outline for a student-led project on creating an interactive website about endangered species."
  - **Supporting Material:** "Generate a step-by-step guide for students planning to organize a charity event in their community."
  - **Event Planning:** "Propose a comprehensive plan for a science fair project examining the effects of different fertilizers on plant growth."
  - **Brainstorming Projects:** "Design a project for a history class where students learn about their local community's history through project-based learning."
- Student Prompts
  - **Planning:** "I want to design a mobile app for a school project. What are the steps I should follow from idea to implementation?"

- **Brainstorming:** "Suggest science projects that demonstrate the principles of renewable energy."

- **Designing:** "How can I create a project that explores the impact of social media on teenagers' mental health?"

- **Feedback:** "What considerations should I keep in mind when planning a project to create a short film about the importance of recycling? Here is what I have so far: {fill}."

BLOOM'S TAXONOMY AND CRITICAL THINKING SKILLS IN THE AI-ENHANCED CLASSROOM

- How can Bloom's Taxonomy be applied to AI-enhanced learning experiences?

- How can AI support learning objectives based on Bloom's Taxonomy?

- How can AI tools help students reach higher levels of Bloom's Taxonomy?

Bloom's Taxonomy, a framework for categorizing educational goals, helps educators think about the cognitive complexity of tasks, ensuring that they build up to the highest levels by gradually increasing the complexity of students' understanding of the target material. While this approach is widely accepted, it requires intensive planning and preparation to scaffold material for each level. AI can help reduce the workload by assisting students to move from understanding basic concepts to applying them in complex problem-solving scenarios.

At the same time, Bloom's Taxonomy can also frame how students can productively use AI in classrooms.

To incorporate Bloom's Taxonomy into how we think about AI integration, teachers can consider the following:

- **Aligning learning objectives:** Use Bloom's Taxonomy to create clear learning objectives for AI activities.
- **Designing activities:** Target different levels of cognitive complexity with each AI activity.
- **Assessing learning:** Evaluate students' performances by considering content knowledge and cognitive processes during AI activities.
- **Facilitating reflection:** Help students reflect on their learning by encouraging them to identify the cognitive processes they engaged in during AI activities.

As AI technology adapts and specific education technology solutions keep emerging, Bloom's Taxonomy will likely be integrated into learning platforms. For example, a learning platform might target different levels of Bloom's Taxonomy based on the individual learners' needs and progress. This would allow them to tailor learning activities to students' cognitive abilities and help students engage with content and tasks at the appropriate level of cognitive complexity.

In addition, AI tools can also augment traditional classroom learning that aligns with Bloom's Taxonomy and reduce teacher workload. For example, teachers can use AI tools to:

- **Adapt content:** AI tools can adjust the complexity and cognitive demands of learning materials in alignment with specific levels of Bloom's Taxonomy.

- **Scaffold resources:** AI chatbots can suggest supplementary activities that help students progress through different levels of Bloom's Taxonomy.

- **Generate formative feedback:** AI systems can generate personalized feedback for students, target specific levels of Bloom's Taxonomy, and provide guidance for improvement and progression.

- **Assess design:** AI tools can help educators design assessments that align with Bloom's Taxonomy depending on the educator's goals.

- **Create learning pathways:** AI-driven platforms can create personalized learning pathways that guide students through progressively more complex cognitive tasks aligned with Bloom's Taxonomy.

Most of this chapter also provides suggestions for how teachers can target particular levels of Bloom's Taxonomy using AI through prompts or new tools. The following activities, which are discussed elsewhere, can help target students develop higher-order thinking skills:

- **Inquiry-based learning:** AI can support inquiry-based learning experiences by encouraging students to engage in higher-order thinking skills such as analysis, evaluation, and synthesis.

- **Problem- and project-based learning:** AI can help create simulations and real-world scenarios to provide opportunities for students to apply higher-level cognitive processes in solving complex problems.

- **Active learning:** AI tools can offer metacognitive guidance and reflection prompts so that students develop awareness and control of their higher-order thinking processes.

As AI takes over lower-order thinking skills, we must ensure students are equipped with higher-order skills to keep up with the pace of AI development. Ensuring that students can evaluate and create effectively will ensure they can think critically about AI outputs and generate unique, creative outputs of their own.

Prompt It!

REMEMBERING

- Teacher Prompts
  - **Test Recall:** "Develop a quiz that tests students' ability to recall the key historical events leading up to World War II."
  - **Aid Memorization:** "Create flashcards that help students remember the key terms in a specific scientific field."
  - **Isolate Key Details:** "Design a worksheet that asks students to list the main characters and their attributes in a novel."
  - **Matching:** "Develop an activity where students match mathematical formulas to their names."
- Student Prompts
  - **Self-Assessment:** "Generate a quiz to help me remember the key historical events leading up to World War II."
  - **Study Aid:** "Create flashcards to help me memorize the important terms in cellular biology."
  - **Summarize Key Details:** "Describe the main characters and their roles in the book *To Kill a Mockingbird*."

UNDERSTANDING

- Teacher Prompts

  - **Design Lessons:** "Design a lesson plan that encourages students to paraphrase the theory of evolution."

  - **Facilitate Discussion:** "Create a group discussion around interpreting the main themes in a piece of literature."

  - **Test Comprehension:** "Develop an assignment asking students to explain the concept of democracy in their own words."

- Student Prompts

  - **Seek Clarity:** "Explain the theory of evolution in simple terms."

  - **Self-Assessment:** "Create short-response questions for me to learn the concept of democracy and its importance."

APPLYING

- Teacher Prompts

  - **Real-World Applications:** "Develop an assignment where students use the principles of physics to solve a real-world problem."

  - **Role-Plays:** "Design a lesson plan that involves students using a foreign language to conduct a mock business meeting."

  - **Projects:** "Create a project where students apply the scientific method to test a hypothesis."

- **Practice Worksheets:** "Create an assignment that asks students to apply grammar rules to correct sentences."
- Student Prompts
  - **Contextualize:** "Provide examples of real-world problems that can be solved using the principles of physics."
  - **Scaffold Application:** "How can I use the scientific method to test a hypothesis about plant growth?"

ANALYZING
- Teacher Prompts
  - **Lesson Design:** "Design a lesson plan that requires students to compare and contrast different economic systems."
  - **Material Creation:** "Develop an assignment where students dissect a scientific paper."
  - **Scaffold:** "Develop an activity where students break down a complex math problem into smaller, manageable parts."
- Student Prompts
  - **Study Aid:** "Provide examples that might help me analyze the motivations of the character Macbeth in Shakespeare's play."
  - **Socratic Dialogue:** "Help me analyze the impact of climate change on different ecosystems by asking me questions."

EVALUATING

- Teacher Prompts

    - **Lesson Plan:** "Create a lesson plan where students critically evaluate different sources of information for a research project."

    - **Assessments:** "Develop an assignment asking students to form an opinion on a controversial topic and justify their viewpoint."

    - **Debate:** "Design a group discussion that requires students to debate the ethical implications of genetic modification."

- Student Prompts

    - **Checklist:** "Provide a checklist for critically evaluating sources for a research paper."

    - **Multiple Viewpoints:** "Provide arguments for and against a controversial topic like genetic modification."

    - **Modeling:** "Give examples of how to evaluate the effectiveness of a digital marketing strategy."

CREATING

- Teacher Prompts

    - **Assessment Design:** "Develop an assessment where students design their own experiment to apply the knowledge from this unit."

    - **Lesson Plan:** "Design a lesson plan where students develop a business plan for a startup."

- Student Prompts
  - **Scaffolding:** "Guide me through designing a simple experiment to test gravity."
  - **Study Aid:** "Help me understand how to create my own geometry problems and solutions."

DIFFERENTIATED INSTRUCTION: AI-GENERATED CUSTOMIZED ACTIVITIES

- How can AI help educators identify students' strengths and weaknesses?
- How can AI be used to differentiate classroom learning experiences?
- How can AI support the creation of inclusive learning environments?

Teachers need help to keep up with the different needs of their students, and as class sizes continue to increase, differentiated instruction is becoming ever more complex. Luckily, AI models can customize and personalize content so that teachers can quickly differentiate it and ensure they meet every student's unique needs.

The first step in effective differentiation is the ability to measure each student's strengths and weaknesses. While traditional assessment aims to do just that, teachers rarely have the time to assess every student often enough and thoroughly enough to form a realistic picture of their needs. As AI platforms become more embedded into classrooms, teachers will have tools that will be able to do a lot of that work for them. For example, AI tools might be able to analyze students' writing, identify patterns and trends in their performance, and suggest follow-up resources and assignments to help them develop their skills. Soon, dynamic assessments and diagnostics driven by AI will adapt the questioning and content to pinpoint students' specific skills gaps and areas for improvement. Until then, the current models can quickly analyze student work and identify particular areas for growth unique to each student.

Teachers can also directly use AI to guide their classroom instruction and help create materials to cater their teaching to individual needs. Some ways teachers can use AI for differentiation are:

- **Personalized content:** They can provide draft content and have AI generate customized learning materials and activities catering to students' needs and preferences.

- **Learning pathways:** Teachers can work with AI to create different learning pathways for students that consist of various activities to help students learn the target material based on their interests and preferences.

- **Grouping strategies:** Teachers can provide context about their classroom and have AI suggest effective heterogeneous or homogeneous groups depending on the activity type.

Teachers can also integrate AI tools built for classrooms to tailor student learning pathways in real time. For example, AI tools can gradually increase the complexity of learning tasks based on performance, while also providing timely support and resources to help students overcome specific challenges as they encounter them. The "just in time" nature of the feedback helps create a continuous feedback loop for students to gain insight into their individual performance and needs quicker than an individual teacher can provide it. Finally, if students struggle with classwork, they can turn to AI to generate examples or hints to have something to model their own work on.

Differentiation needs extend beyond helping students who are at different points in their own learning journeys. It is also necessary to create inclusive and accessible classroom spaces. Like the customization possible for general differentiation, AI can help teachers adapt lessons and content to be more accessible. For example:

- **Accessibility:** AI tools can adapt content based on individual learning needs, including text-to-speech and speech-to-text software.

- **Personalization:** AI can be used to rewrite content at different reading levels so that students can focus on learning the content.

- **Multilingual support:** AI can provide real-time translation and language support for classroom activities, assessments, and homework.

- **Cultural sensitivity:** Teachers can also use AI tools as one component of ensuring cultural sensitivity by cross-checking classroom materials for culturally insensitive material.

Given these capabilities, AI is an effective tool for implementing universal design for learning (UDL). For example, it can help teachers implement all three tiers of UDL:

- **Multiple Means of Representation:** AI can generate content in different modalities (images, tabular, auditory, diagrams, text, etc.) to meet different learning styles.

- **Multiple Means of Action and Expression:** AI can help teachers generate new ideas to provide students with various options to demonstrate their understanding of the content.

- **Multiple Means of Engagement:** AI can customize assignments and content to match students' interests and offer choices and resources depending on their individual learning profile.

Prompt It!

- Teacher Prompts

    - **Creating Differentiated Assignments:** "Generate three versions of a math problem set, each tailored to different skill levels: beginner, intermediate, and advanced."

    - **Lesson Plan Adaptation:** "Provide a differentiated lesson plan on the topic of the water cycle, suitable for students with varying learning styles: visual, auditory, and kinesthetic."

    - **Inclusive Learning Material:** "Design an interactive storytelling activity that incorporates elements of auditory, visual, and tactile learning to ensure inclusivity for students with different learning preferences and abilities."

    - **Identifying Student Strengths:** "Propose a set of formative assessment activities that can help me identify the unique strengths and weaknesses in my students' understanding of the concept of photosynthesis."

    - **Engagement for All:** "Create a classroom game that supports learning about the American Revolution. The game should have different roles and tasks suitable for students with varying learning abilities and styles."

    - **Flexible Grouping:** "Suggest a classroom activity for a biology lesson on cell division that allows for flexible grouping based on the students' familiarity with the topic."

- Student Prompts
  - **Self-Paced Learning:** "Explain the basics of Algebra in simple terms, then provide me with an intermediate-level problem to solve. If I solve it correctly, give me a more complex problem. If I fail, provide a simpler problem."
  - **Interactive Learning:** "I'm a visual learner. Can you explain the concept of the solar system with the help of a descriptive, interactive story?"
  - **Reinforcing Knowledge:** "Based on my understanding of the Civil War, give me a quiz to test my knowledge. If I score high, give me more advanced questions. If I score low, give me easier questions to reinforce the basic concepts."
  - **Learning through Application:** "I just learned about Pythagoras' theorem. Can you provide me with real-world applications or problems using this theorem?"
  - **Inclusive Learning:** "I have dyslexia. Can you explain the structure of a DNA molecule in a way that's easy for me to understand?"
  - **Guided Practice:** "I'm struggling with the concept of chemical reactions. Could you walk me through an example, step by step?"
  - **Understanding through Analogies:** "I'm a kinesthetic learner. Can you explain the concept of gravity using an analogy or a physical activity I can try at home?"
  - **Enrichment Activity:** "I've mastered the basics of coding in Python. Can you give me a challenging project to work on that will help me apply and expand my skills?"

FOSTERING COLLABORATION AND RELATIONSHIP-BUILDING THROUGH AI INTEGRATION

- Why is collaborative and relationship-building-based education key in an age of AI?

- How can AI tools support collaboration and relationship-building in the classroom?

- How can AI support the development of empathy and social skills in students?

We've previously discussed the importance of nurturing and enhancing human relationships as technology, especially AI, assumes a growing role in our lives. As AI transforms the nature of work, students must focus on honing their interpersonal skills to thrive in this new environment. This approach is where collaborative learning becomes valuable. It encourages students to develop their critical thinking and problem-solving abilities. In a group dynamic, students learn to articulate their viewpoints, defend their ideas, and negotiate compromises with their peers. This focus on collaboration and relationship-building also promotes the development of empathy, communication, and social skills, providing students with practical experience in working together toward a common goal.

AI tools will likely become core components of collaborative learning environments and serve as guides for students to engage in productive discussions and teamwork. For example, AI could keep track of what contributions each student is making, and provide feedback afterward about how much they spoke, what kinds of insights they provided, and where their strengths and weaknesses are in a group setting. They could facilitate the group discussion by adding questions or remarks to help move the conversation along and even respond to something a student says that might be incorrect or off-topic. Until AI tools can be integrated directly into our classrooms, teachers can use AI to develop innovative ways to encourage collaboration in their classrooms, and students can use AI to practice cooperation and conversing on difficult topics by chatting with it as if they were in a group setting.

AI may not be sentient yet, but it can mimic sentience enough through language to help students work on their socioemotional skills. For example, AI can help roleplay conversations and discussions in interactive activities and simulations by creating scenarios for teachers to use or by directly being embedded into games and interactive websites. AI can also help students see multiple perspectives by facilitating perspective-taking exercises and encouraging students to consider the viewpoints of others to develop empathy and understanding.

Prompt It!

COLLABORATION

- Teacher Prompts

  - **Classroom Guide:** "Generate a step-by-step guide on how to conduct a collaborative group project on the themes in *Romeo and Juliet*."

  - **Options:** "Create a list of activities that a small group might use to reinforce the material they learned about the American Revolutionary War."

  - **Guideposts:** "Develop a series of questions for a peer review session that will promote constructive feedback and collaboration."

  - **Guidelines:** "Develop a set of guidelines for online team projects to foster collaboration."

  - **Prompts:** "Draft a series of discussion prompts that foster collaboration during literature circles."

- Student Prompts

  - **Problem-Solving**: "My teammate isn't doing their share of the work. How can I approach it?"

  - **Ideas:** "How can my friends and I practice multiplication together in a fun way?"

  - **Coaching:** "Can you help me understand how to convince my peers of my opinion during this group project?"

RELATIONSHIP-BUILDING

- Teacher Prompts

  - **Icebreakers:** "Create a series of icebreaker activities that will help to build relationships among middle school students."

  - **Questions:** "Draft a series of discussion questions that can be used to foster teacher-student relationships during a one-on-one conversation."

  - **Curricular Integration:** "Design a group activity that encourages relationship-building among students while also teaching them about the history of the Renaissance."

  - **Cultural Exchange:** "Design an activity that promotes relationship-building through a shared exploration of cultures and traditions."

- Student Prompts

  - **Coaching:** "What are some good ways to foster a positive relationship with my teacher?"

  - **Coaching:** "I keep getting into a fight with my friend about sharing toys; how can I avoid upsetting them?"

DEVELOPMENT OF EMPATHY AND SOCIAL SKILLS

- Teacher Prompts
    - **Role-Play:** "Create a series of role-play scenarios that can be used to teach empathy and social skills."
    - **Books:** "Generate a list of book recommendations that can be used to teach students about empathy and social skills."
    - **Storytelling:** "Generate a lesson plan that utilizes storytelling about a historical event to help students empathize."
    - **Perspective-Taking:** "Design a classroom project that encourages students to explore the different perspectives in literature through letters between characters."
- Student Prompts
    - **Blindspot:** "Here is what I have written about my opinion so far. What am I not considering?"
    - **Simulations:** "Create a hypothetical situation and help me understand how I could respond empathetically."
    - **Role-Play:** "Role-play as someone from history and help me understand the event from their perspective."

INQUIRY-BASED LEARNING AND AI: ENCOURAGING STUDENT-CENTERED EXPLORATION

- Why is inquiry-based learning important for the future of education?
- How can teachers use AI to encourage inquiry-based learning?
- How can AI help students pursue their own explorations?

Students will need to be curious and inquisitive in order to make the most of the resources that AI provides them. At the most basic level, most generative AI tools require users to inquire to generate proper responses. In the bigger picture, students will need critical thinking skills to effectively analyze and question the content or even decisions that AI generates. Being able to ask the right questions will allow students to get the right resources and information to achieve their goals. Inquiry-based learning also inherently shifts the focus to the student's own learning journeys, which helps foster the curiosity, growth mindset, and autonomy necessary to continuously adapt to the changing world.

Using AI chatbots to explore topics or have meaningful conversations will alone help students begin to think about learning as inquiring. Additional tools built with AI are likely to help students more directly approach inquiry-based learning:

- **Research assistants:** Tools that help students find relevant resources and information for their inquiries and suggest next steps.

- **Socratic dialogue tools:** AI bots that generate open-ended questions to stimulate student curiosity and exploration.

- **Simulation software:** AI-powered simulations and virtual environments will enable students to explore real-world scenarios and test hypotheses.

Teachers can also use AI to help draft scaffolds and prompts to provoke and instigate student thinking. For example, educators can feed content to the AI and have it generate relevant open-ended questions by identifying key concepts within learning materials. AI can also create a range of questions or exploration paths based on student interests and learning preferences. For example, a teacher might ask an AI bot to create a list of books that explore the theme of Bildungsroman but from different periods and settings.

Students can also rely directly on AI tools to help them on their learning journeys. By practicing asking the right questions to gain the information and resources they need, they can begin to internalize the importance of inquiry in intellectual growth. Students can use AI as:

- **Research assistance:** AI tools can help students find, evaluate, and organize relevant sources.

- **Text summarization:** AI can generate concise summaries of complex texts to help students digest information.

- **Data analysis:** AI can help students analyze and interpret data and point out gaps or interesting next steps for their projects.

- **Guided brainstorming:** AI can provide suggestions to help students generate their own questions and hypotheses.

- **Feedback on questions:** AI can offer feedback on the quality and relevance of topics, questions, and hypotheses that students generate to ensure they start their explorations effectively.

- **Modeling question generation:** AI can model effective question generation by providing different examples.

- **Cross-curricular integration:** AI can help point out connections between subject areas to help students ask interdisciplinary questions.

AI tools can serve as personal companions for students while they embark on their learning explorations. Teachers can also rely on AI to customize assignments and projects to better suit their students' curiosities.

Prompt It!

- Teacher Prompts

  - **Create a Role-Playing Activity:** "Generate a role-playing activity that will help students understand the struggles and triumphs of the key figures during the American Civil War."

  - **Design a Science Experiment:** "Develop an experiment that can help students understand the concept of photosynthesis. Include guiding questions encouraging students to predict outcomes, make observations, and reflect on results."

  - **Explore Historical Perspectives:** "Design a lesson plan that encourages students to explore the different perspectives of key stakeholders during the signing of the Magna Carta."

  - **Critical Thinking in Literature:** "Create a set of discussion questions for a novel that encourage students to critically analyze the main character's motivations."

  - **Understand the Water Cycle:** "Generate an interactive lesson plan that helps students understand the water cycle, involving them in predicting, observing, and explaining various stages."

  - **Math in Daily Life:** "Create a lesson plan that helps students identify and solve real-life mathematical problems in their everyday lives."

  - **Study of Microorganisms:** "Develop an investigation project about the role of microorganisms in our environment. What guiding questions can I provide to help them in their research?"

- Student Prompts
  - **Understanding:** "Can you describe the different types of ecosystems and provide examples of the organisms that live in each?"
  - **Contextualize:** "Can you explain the concept of chemical reactions with an everyday life example?"
  - **Literary Analysis:** "Can you ask me questions about the book so that I can think about the themes and characters in the novel *To Kill a Mockingbird*?"
  - **Independent Learning:** "Can you help me understand the basics of Python coding and guide me in writing a simple program?"

CONCLUSION

Integrating AI into educational systems is a sign of the resilience and evolution of pedagogical theory. This transformation marks a significant shift in education, and within this change, we have found opportunities to enhance our existing practices and, thus, better achieve our educational goals.

AI provides a promising path to address enduring educational challenges, particularly those related to student engagement. Through its capacity to personalize learning experiences and bolster interactivity and immersion, AI holds the potential to boost the efficiency and effectiveness of instruction while concurrently catering to the individual needs of students.

The intersection of AI and pedagogy opens an avenue for the evolution of a range of learning theories, such as the constructivist, behaviorist, and sociocultural approaches. Second, it supports active learning in the classroom, heightening student engagement and motivation. Third, it provides resources for teachers to pursue problem- and project-based learning strategies, leading to more collaborative and dynamic environments. Finally, AI offers the ability to truly differentiate instruction by catering to the diverse learning needs of our students.

AI is not just a tool, but a catalyst for a paradigm shift in education. It can enable what once seemed impossible to become a reality in our classrooms by increasing our capacity to implement interventions effectively. In addition, AI can guide student collaboration and relationship-building and support inquiry-based learning by supporting student-centered exploration.

The adaptation of pedagogy for AI integration is not just desirable but necessary. Through this blending of the old and the new, we can unlock AI's full potential in enhancing learning outcomes and experiences and usher in a new age of learning that is more engaging, personalized, and effective.

Exit Ticket

This chapter has plenty of prompts for you to brainstorm from. First, pick one of the pedagogical approaches and draft prompts for your curriculum. Can you combine multiple different ones for a single lesson plan or unit? Is there one you see yourself using repeatedly?

Chapter 5

Using AI in Curriculum Development

Generative AI tools have the potential to dramatically reduce the amount of time teachers spend creating and revising materials for their classrooms. The amount of time freed from generating lesson plans, creating essential questions, constructing worksheets, assigning homework, building assessments, and making resources will allow teachers to focus on direct instruction.

While time saved is a significant advantage, it is not the only reason to use AI for curriculum development. The content generated by AI can be customized quickly, adapted to current events, personalized based on classroom needs and preferences, and match formats and guidelines from administrators. Teachers can also have AI tweak existing content to better align with educational standards and learning objectives and incorporate more perspectives and resources. AI can also be a brainstorming buddy and help develop new ideas, techniques, projects, and activities for teachers to incorporate. The variety of content that AI can generate also makes it helpful in creating multi-modal resources, such as presentations with graphics and text, videos with narrating characters, and auto-generated podcasts for students.

The potential of AI to dramatically shift how teachers prepare for instructional time is apparent, and the rest of the chapter provides specific examples and tips for educators to start incorporating AI into their workflow.

LESSON PLANNING AND CURRICULAR DESIGN

- How can AI help teachers create efficient and effective lesson plans?

- How can AI improve the quality and relevance of instructional materials?

- How can AI be used to align curriculum with learning standards and goals?

Generative AI has the ability to help teachers quickly create lesson plans that meet the needs of their unique classrooms. Because the AI systems are able to respond to the text provided to them, they have the ability to generate hyperspecific and unique lesson plans depending on the kinds of things educators ask the AI to generate. The AI can help develop a template, or teachers can suggest their own, and it can be customized toward different subjects, grade levels, and even instructional approaches. The AI systems have already been trained on a range of standards, but teachers can also provide their own and have the AI tools create assignments based on those standards.

While the AI might not generate the perfect lesson plan on the first attempt, teachers can ask it to modify things and then put the finishing touches on it themselves! In addition, with the time saved by having draft lesson plans generated by AI, educators can spend more time refining and implementing them in their classrooms.

Here, we'll walk through an example highlighting a few key features of AI-generated lesson plans.

Basic Prompt

Prompt: "For a 9th-grade AP World History classroom, generate a lesson plan for a 45-minute class on the green revolution in India."

In this prompt, I start with basic information about the class (grade level and subject area), the amount of time I have, and the specific topic I want to cover. From that, ChatGPT, my tool of choice for this example, produces the following lesson plan:

As shown in Figure 5.1, ChatGPT knew what the basic layout of a good lesson plan might be, broke down the lesson into smaller chunks, and even suggested some extension activities. This would be a great starting place for me to plan a lesson!

Prompt with Template

Now, suppose you want to get the output in a table format, and you want guiding questions, standards, a door opener, a lecture, a group activity, and an exit ticket as the format of your lesson. In that case, you can modify your prompt to specify all that.

Prompt: "For a 5th-grade English class, generate a lesson plan for a 30-minute class on subject-verb agreement with guiding questions, common core standards, a door opener, lecture, group activity, and an exit ticket, all in a table format."

In Figure 5.2, you can see that ChatGPT formatted the lesson plan according to my requirements, including the relevant standards.

Lesson Title: The Green Revolution in India: Catalyst of Change

Grade Level: 9th Grade (AP World History)

Lesson Duration: 45 Minutes

Learning Objectives:

- Understand the background and significance of the Green Revolution in India.
- Identify key figures, technologies, and policies that contributed to the Green Revolution.
- Analyze the impacts of the Green Revolution on Indian society, economy, and environment.
- Evaluate the successes and criticisms of the Green Revolution.

Materials Needed:

- Computer with internet access and projector
- PowerPoint presentation on the Green Revolution in India
- Handout of key terms and figures
- Short documentary or video clip on the Green Revolution
- Whiteboard and markers

Lesson Plan:

1. Introduction (5 minutes)

- Begin by asking students if they know what the Green Revolution is. Take a couple of responses to gauge students' prior knowledge.
- Briefly explain the concept of the Green Revolution and its significance, mentioning its focus on agricultural production and its global impact.

2. Presentation (10 minutes)

- Use a PowerPoint presentation to provide an overview of the Green Revolution in India. Cover the following topics:
  - Background: Post-colonial India's food scarcity and dependence on foreign aid.
  - Key Figures: M. S. Swaminathan, Norman Borlaug, and others.
  - Introduction of High Yield Variety (HYV) seeds.
  - Implementation of new farming techniques and use of chemical fertilizers and pesticides.

Figure 5.1 ChatGPT output of a lesson plan with learning objectives, materials, a broken down lesson plan, homework, and assessment ideas.

3. Video and Discussion (10 minutes)

* Show a short documentary or video clip about the Green Revolution in India. This should provide a visual representation of the changes brought by the revolution.
* After the video, facilitate a brief discussion. Ask questions like: "What surprised you about the video?" or "What impacts of the Green Revolution were depicted in the video?"

4. Impact Analysis (10 minutes)

* Divide the class into small groups and assign each group one aspect of the Green Revolution's impact to analyze: societal, economic, or environmental.
* Ask each group to come up with two positive and two negative impacts in their assigned area, using the information learned so far and their handouts.

5. Group Sharing and Class Discussion (8 minutes)

* Invite each group to present their findings to the class. Encourage other students to ask questions or add comments.
* Facilitate a discussion around the question: "Do you think the Green Revolution was more beneficial or detrimental to India?"

6. Conclusion (2 minutes)

* Summarize the key points discussed during the lesson.
* Emphasize the complexity of the Green Revolution's impacts and how it played a major role in shaping modern India.

Homework Assignment:

* Ask students to write a one-page reflection paper on the question: "Given the benefits and drawbacks of the Green Revolution, would you have supported it if you were a policymaker in the 1960s? Why or why not?"

Assessment:

* Class participation in group work and discussion
* Homework reflection paper

Extensions:

* For students interested in exploring further, recommend resources on related topics like the current state of agriculture in India, the role of women in the Green Revolution, or the comparison between the Green Revolution in India and other countries.

Figure 5.1 *(Continued)*

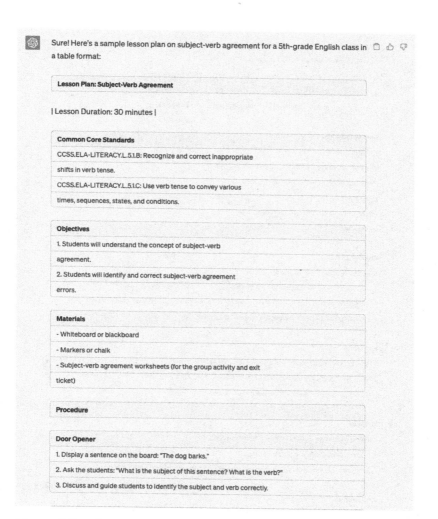

Sure! Here's a sample lesson plan on subject-verb agreement for a 5th-grade English class in a table format:

Lesson Plan: Subject-Verb Agreement

| Lesson Duration: 30 minutes |

Common Core Standards

CCSS.ELA-LITERACY.L.5.1.B: Recognize and correct inappropriate shifts in verb tense.

CCSS.ELA-LITERACY.L.5.1.C: Use verb tense to convey various times, sequences, states, and conditions.

Objectives

1. Students will understand the concept of subject-verb agreement.

2. Students will identify and correct subject-verb agreement errors.

Materials

- Whiteboard or blackboard

- Markers or chalk

- Subject-verb agreement worksheets (for the group activity and exit ticket)

Procedure

Door Opener

1. Display a sentence on the board: "The dog barks."

2. Ask the students: "What is the subject of this sentence? What is the verb?"

3. Discuss and guide students to identify the subject and verb correctly.

Figure 5.2 ChatGPT output of a lesson plan in a table format, with all the requested components.

Lecture

1. Explain subject-verb agreement using examples.

2. Discuss how the subject and verb must agree in number (singular or plural).

3. Highlight common errors, such as using plural verbs with singular subjects.

4. Provide strategies for identifying the subject and selecting the correct verb.

Guiding Questions

- What is subject-verb agreement?

- How do we identify the subject and verb?

- Why is it important for subjects and verbs to

agree in number?

- What are some common errors in subject-verb

agreement?

Group Activity

1. Divide the class into small groups.

2. Distribute subject-verb agreement worksheets.

3. Instruct students to identify and correct subject-verb agreement errors in the sentences provided.

4. Encourage collaboration and discussion within the groups.

Exit Ticket

1. Hand out individual subject-verb agreement worksheets.

2. Students should complete the sentences by choosing the correct verb form.

3. Collect the exit tickets to assess student understanding.

Wrap-up

1. Review the correct answers to the exit ticket as a class.

2. Address any questions or misconceptions.

3. Summarize the importance of subject-verb agreement and its role in clear communication.

Assessment

- Group activity participation and corrections.

- Exit ticket completion and accuracy.

Note: You can adapt and modify the lesson plan according to your specific classroom needs and time constraints.

↻ Regenerate response

Figure 5.2 *(Continued)*

Prompt with Teaching Style

Perhaps you've taken the last few chapters to heart and want to ensure you incorporate project-based learning in your classroom. Then, you can similarly include that in your initial prompt.

Prompt: "For a 3rd-grade science class, generate a lesson plan for a 60-minute lesson that incorporates project-based learning to teach the concept of gravity based on common core standards."

Similarly, as shown in Figure 5.3, ChatGPT is able to create a lesson plan that matches the teaching style I suggested and provides suggestions for a project to teach the concept of gravity.

As you begin to use ChatGPT or other similar platforms, you will come up with your own set of prompts that consistently get you the closest to the lesson plans you want. We have included more prompts in the following, but you should also experiment with your own!

The last example clarifies the potential of AI in helping teachers do work faster and develop innovative ways to teach their students. For example, you can ask for lesson plans that use active learning, lesson plans that address all Bloom's Taxonomy stages, or inquiry-based learning suggestions. You can also ask the AI tools to scaffold a topic clearly or customize the lesson plan. Some examples are provided in the following.

For all of these exercises, you can also provide the AI tools with what you already have and ask it to adapt or modify it based on your needs. For example, provide a lesson plan and ask it to provide four different assessment options so that your students have some flexibility. You can also incorporate student feedback and voice into your lesson planning by relaying feedback to the AI tools.

Prompt with Feedback

Prompt: "My students found my last classroom activity to be too static; they want something where they can move around. Generate a 45-minute lesson plan for one-digit multiplication for my 3rd-grade classroom, incorporating that feedback." (See Figure 5.4.)

Lesson Title: Exploring Gravity through Project-Based Learning

Grade Level: 3rd Grade

Duration: 60 minutes

Objective: Students will understand the concept of gravity and its effects on objects by engaging in a project-based learning activity.

Materials Needed:

- Small objects (marbles, balls, paper clips, feathers, etc.)
- String or thread
- Paper
- Pencils
- Rulers
- Sticky notes
- Whiteboard or chalkboard
- Markers or chalk
- Optional: Books or online resources about gravity

Lesson Plan:

Introduction (5 minutes):

1. Begin the lesson by asking students if they know what keeps their feet on the ground and objects from floating away.
2. Discuss their responses and introduce the concept of gravity as a force that pulls objects towards each other.
3. Write the word "Gravity" on the board and explain that today's lesson will be all about exploring this force and its effects.

Activity 1: Gravity Investigation (20 minutes):

1. Divide the students into small groups of 3-4 students each.
2. Provide each group with a variety of small objects.
3. Instruct the groups to predict which objects will fall to the ground faster and which ones will take longer to fall.
4. Encourage students to discuss their predictions within their groups.
5. Distribute string or thread to each group and have them tie one end to a small object.
6. Instruct the students to hold the other end of the string at shoulder height and drop the object.
7. Students should observe and discuss the results within their groups, comparing their predictions to the actual outcomes.
8. As a class, discuss the observat [Regenerate response] gs on the board or chart paper.

Figure 5.3 ChatGPT output with two project-based activities appropriate for a 3rd-grade science class.

Activity 2: Gravity Experiments (25 minutes):

1. Explain that students will now conduct a series of gravity experiments to further explore the concept.
2. Divide the class into pairs and provide each pair with paper, pencils, rulers, and sticky notes.
3. Instruct the pairs to design and conduct their experiments to investigate gravity.
   - For example, they can test the time it takes for different objects to fall from the same height, the effect of weight on falling speed, or the effect of surface area on falling objects.
4. Encourage students to make predictions, perform the experiments, and record their observations and findings on the paper.
5. Circulate around the room to assist and guide the students as needed.
6. After the experiments, gather the class together and ask each pair to share their experiment, observations, and conclusions.
7. Facilitate a class discussion to consolidate the learning and highlight key findings.

Conclusion (10 minutes):

1. Recap the main points discussed during the lesson and emphasize the role of gravity in our daily lives.
2. Ask students to reflect on what they have learned about gravity and share any new insights or questions they have.
3. Summarize the importance of project-based learning in deepening understanding and promoting hands-on exploration.
4. If time permits, recommend books or online resources about gravity that students can explore at home.
5. Thank the students for their participation and conclude the lesson.

Extension Activity (Optional):
Encourage students to create posters or drawings that depict real-life examples of gravity and its effects. They can illustrate how gravity affects objects on Earth, the movement of celestial bodies, or the importance of gravity in our daily activities.

Note: The time allocation for each activity is approximate and can be adjusted based on the needs of the class.

Figure 5.3   *(Continued)*

Here, not only did ChatGPT incorporate the feedback, but it provided two different activities that both meet the needs voiced by the students. This allows you to rapidly adapt your classroom to your students' needs without spending hours in between each lesson revamping your plans for the next day.

Title: Multiplication March

Grade Level: 3rd grade
Subject: Mathematics
Duration: 45 minutes

Objective:
By the end of the lesson, students will be able to confidently multiply single-digit numbers and demonstrate their understanding through movement-based activities.

Materials:

1. Chart paper or whiteboard
2. Markers or whiteboard markers
3. Number cards (0-9)
4. Floor tape or cones to mark activity stations

Lesson Plan:

Introduction (5 minutes):

1. Greet the students and explain that today's lesson will involve movement-based activities to make learning multiplication more engaging.
2. Review the concept of multiplication and its basic terms (multiplier, multiplicand, product).
3. Ask students to share any strategies they currently use for multiplying single-digit numbers.

Activity 1: Multiplication Relay Race (15 minutes):

1. Divide the students into groups of 4-5.
2. Set up stations using floor tape or cones, each labeled with a different multiplication equation (e.g., 2 × 3, 4 × 5, etc.).
3. Provide each group with a set of number cards (0-9).
4. Explain that one student from each group will start at their designated station with a number card in hand.
5. On your signal, the students will solve the multiplication equation using their number card and run to the next station.
6. At the next station, they will find a missing number card and complete the equation. They will then hand the completed equation to the next student in their group.
7. Repeat the process until all students have completed the relay race.
8. Encourage students to cheer for their teammates and provide positive feedback.

Figure 5.4 ChatGPT output of two activities that incorporate movement into the activities.

Activity 2: Multiplication Hopscotch (15 minutes):

1. Draw a large hopscotch grid on the floor using floor tape or chalk.
2. Label each square with a multiplication equation (e.g., 3 × 4, 5 × 2, etc.).
3. Divide the students into pairs.
4. Explain that each pair will take turns tossing a beanbag onto the hopscotch grid.
5. When the beanbag lands on a square, the student must solve the multiplication equation and say the answer aloud.
6. If the answer is correct, the student can hop on the corresponding square and continue their turn.
7. If the answer is incorrect, they lose their turn, and it's the other student's turn.
8. Encourage students to use different strategies for solving the equations (e.g., skip counting, repeated addition).

Conclusion (10 minutes):

1. Gather the students together and review the multiplication equations they encountered during the activities.
2. Ask the students to reflect on how movement helped them engage with the concept of multiplication.
3. Discuss any challenges they faced and how they overcame them.
4. Provide opportunities for students to share their favorite moments from the lesson.
5. Summarize the key concepts covered in the lesson and encourage students to continue practicing multiplication skills at home.

Extension:
Assign multiplication-related worksheets or online games for independent practice at home. Encourage students to use movement or physical objects (e.g., counters, beads) to reinforce their understanding of multiplication.

Note: Adapt the lesson plan as needed based on the size of your classroom and the number of students.

Figure 5.4 *(Continued)*

AI tools can also be used to help plan out a curriculum or unit while helping you think about time allocation, standards, and the unique needs that your classroom might have.

Prompt with Backward Design
Prompt: "Using backward design, plan a unit on the theory of relativity for a 10th-grade physics classroom with two weeks to cover the unit." (See Figure 5.5.)

Unit Title: Exploring the Theory of Relativity

Grade Level: 10th grade
Duration: 2 weeks

Unit Overview:
In this unit, students will delve into the fascinating world of the theory of relativity, a cornerstone of modern physics. They will explore both the special and general theories of relativity proposed by Albert Einstein, understanding the profound impact these theories have had on our understanding of space, time, and gravity. Through a combination of engaging activities, discussions, and hands-on experiments, students will develop a deep conceptual understanding of relativity and its implications.

Enduring Understanding:
The theory of relativity revolutionized our understanding of the universe, challenging our intuitions about space, time, and gravity and paving the way for modern physics.

Essential Questions:

1. What are the key principles of the theory of relativity?
2. How do the special and general theories of relativity differ?
3. What are the implications of relativity for our understanding of space, time, and gravity?

Unit Objectives:
By the end of the unit, students will be able to:

1. Describe the basic principles of the theory of relativity.
2. Differentiate between the special and general theories of relativity.
3. Explain the concepts of time dilation and length contraction.
4. Discuss the implications of relativity for our understanding of the universe.
5. Apply the principles of relativity to solve problems and analyze scenarios.

Week 1:

Day 1: Introduction to Relativity

- Engage students with a short video or a thought-provoking question about our intuitive understanding of space and time.
- Introduce the historical context and significance of the theory of relativity.
- Present the enduring understanding and essential questions for the unit.
- Conduct a class discussion to elicit students' prior knowledge and misconceptions.

Figure 5.5 ChatGPT output of a broken-down unit plan by week and day with clear objectives.

Day 2: Special Theory of Relativity

* Introduce the basic principles of the special theory of relativity, including the constancy of the speed of light and the relativity of simultaneity.
* Provide examples and thought experiments to illustrate the concepts.
* Engage students in small group discussions or a gallery walk to explore the implications of special relativity.

Day 3: Time Dilation and Length Contraction

* Explain the concepts of time dilation and length contraction, using real-life examples and analogies.
* Conduct demonstrations or simulations to help students visualize and understand these phenomena.
* Assign practice problems or activities for students to apply their knowledge.

Day 4: Relativistic Momentum and Energy

* Discuss the relationship between mass, momentum, and energy in the context of relativity.
* Present the concept of mass-energy equivalence ($E=mc^2$) and its implications.
* Engage students in problem-solving activities or thought experiments to deepen their understanding.

Day 5: Assessment and Review

* Administer a formative assessment to check students' understanding of the topics covered during the week.
* Review the key concepts and address any misconceptions.
* Provide additional practice problems or review materials for students to reinforce their learning.

Week 2:

Day 1: General Theory of Relativity

* Introduce the general theory of relativity, focusing on the concept of spacetime curvature.
* Discuss the role of gravity and the equivalence principle.
* Engage students in hands-on activities or computer simulations to explore the bending of light and the warping of spacetime.

Figure 5.5 *(Continued)*

Day 2: Black Holes and Gravitational Waves

- Explore the phenomena of black holes and gravitational waves, emphasizing their connection to the general theory of relativity.
- Use visualizations and multimedia resources to enhance understanding.
- Discuss the recent discoveries in the field, such as the detection of gravitational waves.

Day 3: Implications and Applications of Relativity

- Discuss the practical applications of relativity in everyday life, such as GPS systems.
- Explore the philosophical and scientific implications of relativity for our understanding of the universe.
- Engage students in a debate or discussion on controversial topics related to relativity.

Day 4: Historical Perspectives and Famous Experiments

- Present the historical development of the theory of relativity and the key experiments that supported it.
- Show videos or conduct demonstrations of famous experiments like the Michelson-Morley experiment and the Eddington solar eclipse expedition.
- Discuss the role of scientists like Albert Einstein and their contributions to the theory.

Day 5: Unit Reflection and Culminating Project

- Provide time for students to reflect on their learning throughout the unit.
- Assign a culminating project where students can apply their knowledge creatively, such as designing a time travel scenario or creating a multimedia presentation on the impact of relativity.
- Present and share the projects in a class exhibition.

By following this backward design model, you can ensure that students are engaged, develop a deep conceptual understanding of the theory of relativity, and have opportunities to apply their knowledge in real-life contexts.

Figure 5.5 *(Continued)*

Prompt with Standards

Prompt: "I have eight months to prepare my students for the New York State English Regents. Map out my year so that I can cover all the relevant topics and incorporate active learning throughout." (See Figure 5.6.)

With this as a starting point, you could ask ChatGPT for follow-up refinements like a deeper monthly breakdown, an example lesson plan for month 3, or to modify the planning so you have more time to review.

To effectively prepare your students for the New York State English Regents over the course of 8 months, it's important to create a structured plan that covers all the relevant topics while incorporating active learning strategies. Here's a suggested timeline for your year:

Month 1: Introduction to Regents Exam and Diagnostic Assessment

* Familiarize students with the format, requirements, and expectations of the Regents Exam.
* Administer a diagnostic assessment to identify students' strengths and weaknesses.

Months 2-3: Reading Comprehension and Literary Analysis

* Teach strategies for reading comprehension, including close reading and annotation techniques.
* Analyze various literary genres, such as fiction, non-fiction, poetry, and drama.
* Practice identifying and analyzing literary elements (e.g., theme, characterization, symbolism) in sample texts.
* Assign reading assignments and conduct group discussions to encourage active engagement.

Month 4: Argumentative Writing

* Introduce the components of an argumentative essay, including thesis statements, evidence, and counterarguments.
* Teach strategies for developing strong arguments and logical reasoning.
* Practice writing argumentative essays on various topics, incorporating research and evidence.
* Conduct peer review sessions to encourage students to critique and provide feedback on each other's essays.

Month 5: Informative/Explanatory Writing

* Teach the structure and organization of informative/explanatory essays.
* Introduce techniques for conducting research, taking notes, and citing sources.
* Practice writing informative/explanatory essays on topics related to the curriculum.
* Incorporate multimedia sources (articles, videos, podcasts) to enhance student learning.

Figure 5.6 ChatGPT output of a month-by-month plan for the year to study plan for the regents.

Thinking about AI-partnered lesson and curriculum planning as an iterative process will allow you to make the most of it by offloading as much work as possible to the AI. At the same time, you guide it using your experienced understanding of education, your students, and your own teaching style.

Month 6: Literary Analysis Essay

- Review literary analysis techniques from earlier units.
- Teach students how to construct a well-organized and coherent literary analysis essay.
- Provide models of literary analysis essays and discuss effective writing strategies.
- Assign literary analysis essays on selected texts studied throughout the year.

Month 7: Language and Vocabulary Development

- Focus on improving students' language skills, including grammar, syntax, and vocabulary.
- Provide exercises and activities to enhance vocabulary acquisition.
- Analyze sample passages to identify figurative language and rhetorical devices.
- Practice multiple-choice questions related to language and vocabulary on past Regents exams.

Month 8: Review and Exam Preparation

- Review all previously covered topics and address any remaining weaknesses.
- Administer practice exams to familiarize students with the test format and timing.
- Analyze and discuss sample responses to previous exams.
- Provide targeted feedback and individualized support for improvement.

Throughout the Year:

- Integrate active learning strategies such as group discussions, debates, role plays, and project-based assignments.
- Assign regular reading assignments to build students' reading comprehension skills.
- Incorporate technology and digital resources to enhance learning and engagement.
- Offer opportunities for students to reflect on their learning and set personal goals for improvement.

Remember to regularly assess your students' progress through formative and summative assessments and adjust your instruction accordingly. Additionally, provide ongoing support and guidance to individual students who may need extra help.

Figure 5.6   *(Continued)*

Prompt It!

- **Constructivist Approach:** "Design a lesson plan that encourages students to construct their understanding and knowledge of bacteria through experiencing things and reflecting on those experiences."

- **Inquiry-Based Learning:** "Generate a science lesson plan for 8th graders that encourages inquiry-based learning on photosynthesis."

- **Project-Based Learning:** "Design a project-based learning experience for a 6th-grade history class studying Ancient Civilizations. Include the project's goal, steps for implementation, resources required, and evaluation rubrics."

- **Flipped Classroom Model:** "Create a lesson plan for a flipped classroom model in a high school physics class, including pre-class materials, in-class activities, and assessment tools."

- **Montessori Method:** "Describe a Montessori-based lesson plan for kindergarteners focusing on self-directed activity, hands-on learning, and collaborative play."

- **STEAM Education:** "Create a STEAM-based lesson plan for 4th graders to learn about the principles of flight, incorporating aspects of science, technology, engineering, art, and mathematics."

- **Independent Study:** "Design a curriculum for an independent study project for a high school senior on environmental sustainability."

- **Learning Styles:** "Create a lesson plan for a high school geography class that caters to visual, auditory, and kinesthetic learners."

- **Real-World Connections:** "Design a lesson plan for a high school economics class that connects theoretical concepts with real-world examples."

- **Detailed Lesson Plan:** "Generate a detailed lesson plan for teaching the concept of photosynthesis to a 7th-grade science class, including learning objectives, teaching methods, activities, and assessment strategies."

- **Curriculum Plan:** "Describe a comprehensive curriculum plan for an introductory course in Python programming for high school students, ensuring the inclusion of key concepts, projects, and evaluation methods."

- **Unit Plan:** "Provide a detailed sequence of lessons for a unit on Shakespeare's *Romeo and Juliet* for a 10th-grade English literature class, integrating multimedia resources, group activities, and formative assessments."

CREATING LEARNING ASSETS

- What types of learning assets can AI create?
- How can AI be used to create multi-modal learning assets?
- How can students themselves use these AI tools?

Throughout the earlier chapters, I provide plenty of examples and ideas about how to use generative AI to produce text, whether it's worksheets, lesson plans, or quizzes. In this chapter, we focus on the other modes of learning assets that can help you produce. For example, AI can create images, sound, and even videos. You can also use output from AI to work with tools such as Kahoot!

As AI continues to be developed, you will likely be able to use it to generate online simulations, games, and even virtual or augmented reality experiences. But, for now, we focus on practical examples of the possibilities that already exist.

Graphics

You can use various image generation AIs (Midjourney, Stable Diffusion, DALL-E 2, etc.) to create images to use within your classroom.

signing of the declaration of independence in comic book format

U1 U2 U3 U4

V1 V2 V3 V4

Figure 5.7   Midjourney output in Discord with four images in comic style of the signing of the Declaration of Independence.

Everything from presentations and worksheets to posters and custom classroom resources can be enhanced with AI-generated art. For example, if you are working on a comic format for teaching the Declaration of Independence, you might ask Midjourney:

Prompt: "/imagine The signing of the Declaration of Independence in comic book format."

In seconds, MidJourney generates custom images to choose from to use in your project (Figure 5.7).

Tables

You can also have various AI tools create a table for you. For example, you might want to make a *Jeopardy* game and tell Google's Bard:

Prompt: "Can you produce a *Jeopardy* question table with 100-, 200-, 300-, 400-, and 500-dollar questions corresponding to difficulty and five different categories of questions on *To Kill a Mockingbird?*" (See Figure 5.8.)

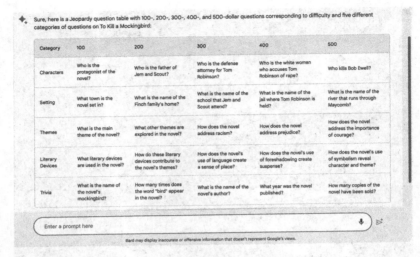

Figure 5.8 Google Bard output of a table with 25 questions in table format.

Sound

Various tools for both text-to-speech and speech-to-text exist that use AI to help move between those two mediums. For example, Speechify can take text and narrate it in fictional voices for a video or presentation you are creating.

In Figure 5.9, ChatGPT was used to make a mock speech (Prompt: "Draft a speech on the Stamp Act.") and then inserted into Speechify to be read in a fake voice.

Presentations

You can draft an entire presentation in a tool like Canva by providing a basic overview of what you want, and then you can modify it based on your lesson plan.

Prompt: "I need a presentation on the Nile River Delta."

In Figure 5.10, Canva creates a draft presentation with relevant pictures, key subtopics, and bullets.

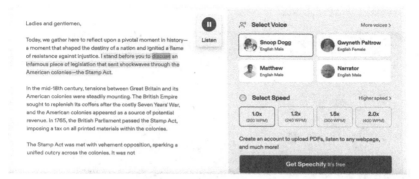

Figure 5.9 Speechify screenshot showing text input box with ChatGPT-generated speech and various options to generate an audio output.

Figure 5.10 Canvas output with slides containing relevant text and images to the Nile River Delta.

Videos

You can use AI systems to create AI videos for a flipped classroom experience. For example, Synthesia lets you import a presentation or

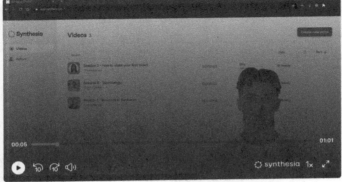

Figure 5.11 Synesthesia screenshot showing AI-generated avatar in a video.

upload a script, and then it will create a video with a voiceover and even a talking avatar for you! (See Figure 5.11.)

You can generate custom avatars, use different voices, and let the AI handle most other steps!

Inputs

There are, of course, education technology tools that you are already familiar with and have used in your classroom. To make it easier to use them, you can use AI tools to create files that you need. For example, you can have ChatGPT make you multiple-choice questions in a table format so that you can import them into your favorite classroom tool (e.g., Kahoot!).

Prompt: "Create 15 multiple-choice questions for a 7th-grade class learning about photosynthesis. The questions will be used in the fun classroom quizzing tool Kahoot! Add a few silly or funny questions in the mix, and provide the questions in a tabular format." (See Figure 5.12.)

Sure, here are some questions and answers about photosynthesis for your 7th grade class. I have included some silly and fun questions as well:

No.	Question	Options	Correct Answer
1	What is photosynthesis?	A) A dance plants do B) Process where plants make food C) Cooking process in plants D) How plants go shopping	B) Process where plants make food
2	Where does photosynthesis take place?	A) In the roots B) In the leaves C) At the supermarket D) In the stems	B) In the leaves
3	What are the main components needed for photosynthesis?	A) Carbon dioxide, water, sunlight B) Water, Oreos, sunlight C) Carbon dioxide, water, moonlight D) Carbon dioxide, soda, sunlight	A) Carbon dioxide, water, sunlight
4	What is the green pigment in plants called that helps them photosynthesize?	A) Chlorophyll B) Greenophyll C) Broccolophyll D) Saladophyll	A) Chlorophyll
5	What is the main product of photosynthesis?	A) Oxygen and Glucose B) Oxygen and Chocolate C) Hydrogen and Glucose D) Oxygen and Bacon	A) Oxygen and Glucose
6	True or False: Photosynthesis only happens during the day.	A) True B) False C) Only on Tuesdays D) Only during full moon	B) False
7	Which gas is used by plants during photosynthesis?	A) Nitrogen B) Carbon Dioxide C) Helium D) Laughing Gas	B) Carbon Dioxide
8	What is the formula for photosynthesis?	A) 6CO2 + 6H2O + Light Energy = C6H12O6 + 6O2 B) H2O + CO2 + Sun = Green plant C) 2CO2 + 3H2O = C2H3 + 2O2 D) Light + Water + Unicorn Dust = Magic Plant	A) 6CO2 + 6H2O + Light Energy = C6H12O6 + 6O2
9	What is the sugar produced by photosynthesis used for?	A) For the plant's food B) For the plant's party on Friday night C) To attract bees D) To make the plant sweeter for herbivores	A) For the plant's food
10	What is the function of stomata in photosynthesis?	A) To help the plant dance B) To help the plant breathe C) To help the plant sleep D) To help the plant sing	B) To help the plant breathe
11	If a plant could speak, what would it say about photosynthesis?	A) "I'm sunbathing!" B) "I'm doing a science experiment!" C) "I'm making lunch!" D) "I'm doing my homework!"	C) "I'm making lunch!"
12	What would happen if a plant doesn't get enough sunlight?	A) It would move to a sunnier location B) It would stop or slow down photosynthesis C) It would order a pizza D) It would start glowing in the dark	B) It would stop or slow down photosynthesis
13	True or False: All parts of a plant can perform photosynthesis.	A) True B) False C) Only the parts that enjoy sunlight D) Only the parts that like green color	B) False
14	What would you call a plant that loves to photosynthesize?	A) Photosynthefreak B) Photosynthefan C) Chlorofill-me-up D) Sunlightoholic	A) Photosynthefreak
15	Why don't plants get sunburnt while photosynthesizing?	A) They wear sunscreen B) They have built-in shade C) They use sunlight productively instead of just absorbing it D) They always carry an umbrella	C) They use sunlight productively instead of just absorbing it

Figure 5.12   ChatGPT output of multiple-choice questions and answers in a table with the answer key.

ChatGPT successfully creates the multiple choice questions, provides the choices (including some funny ones), and provides a format that makes it easy to take to your favorite tool.

Resource Finding

You can also use AI tools that are connected to search engines to find resources that already exist. For example, instead of looking through all the search results for a video on a Supreme Court case, you can ask Bing Chat:

Prompt: "What educational videos are appropriate for a high school classroom on the *Heart of Atlanta Motel, Inc. v. United States* case around 2 minutes in length?"

Not only did Bing provide me with a list of relevant videos, but it also gave me some background information to help me decide between them (Figure 5.13).

Finally, all these tools are effective for teachers who need to create classroom learning assets. However, students can use the same tools

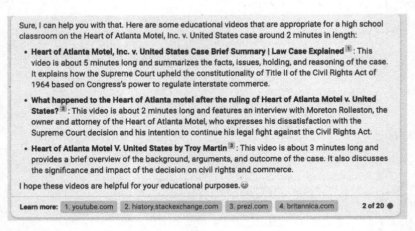

Sure, I can help you with that. Here are some educational videos that are appropriate for a high school classroom on the Heart of Atlanta Motel, Inc. v. United States case around 2 minutes in length:

- **Heart of Atlanta Motel, Inc. v. United States Case Brief Summary | Law Case Explained** [1] : This video is about 5 minutes long and summarizes the facts, issues, holding, and reasoning of the case. It explains how the Supreme Court upheld the constitutionality of Title II of the Civil Rights Act of 1964 based on Congress's power to regulate interstate commerce.
- **What happened to the Heart of Atlanta motel after the ruling of Heart of Atlanta Motel v. United States?** [2] : This video is about 2 minutes long and features an interview with Moreton Rolleston, the owner and attorney of the Heart of Atlanta Motel, who expresses his dissatisfaction with the Supreme Court decision and his intention to continue his legal fight against the Civil Rights Act.
- **Heart of Atlanta Motel V. United States by Troy Martin** [3] : This video is about 3 minutes long and provides a brief overview of the background, arguments, and outcome of the case. It also discusses the significance and impact of the decision on civil rights and commerce.

I hope these videos are helpful for your educational purposes. 😊

Learn more: 1. youtube.com   2. history.stackexchange.com   3. prezi.com   4. britannica.com   2 of 20 ●

Figure 5.13   Bing Chat output with three suggestions for videos with short descriptions of each.

for projects, classroom presentations, and scenarios where they need multi-modal resources. This can serve the dual purpose of ensuring students focus on content rather than style and preparing them for the real world, where they likely won't have to worry about presentation themes and colors. For example, students might use Canva to start their classroom presentations, Descript to edit their podcast, Midjourney to create images for a one-pager or brochure project, and Synthesia to make a PSA.

Also, as a reminder, these are a few examples of the tools and applications that can be used for these purposes. You can see more options and in-depth tutorials on each tool on our website at pedagog.ai.

FORMATIVE ACTIVITIES: GENERATED WORKSHEETS, GAMES, AND MORE

- How can AI generate formative assessments that align with learning objectives?

- How can AI help diversify the kinds of learning activities?

- What kinds of formative activities can AI generate?

Between classroom activities, reinforcement activities, and homework, teachers spend a lot of time creating formative activities for use in their classrooms. Add to that the stress of making new and engaging options and keeping up with curriculum changes, and the entire process can be daunting and time-consuming. Incorporating AI into the workflow can help teachers quickly produce quality activities that students can use to reinforce their learning.

AI tools can consider your learning objectives, specific skills, concepts, and knowledge that need to be reinforced and ensure that they align with any assessments you will use in your classroom. They can also create various learning options so that students have choices when it comes to the activities or so that you can mix up the types of formative activities you are providing. The AI tools can also create answer keys and adaptive exercises to minimize the amount of time teachers need to spend. Many of the example prompts and activities in Chapter 4 can be used to create formative activities, and some more general examples follow.

Suggestions

Prompt: "I'm trying to develop creative and innovative ways to help students learn subject-verb agreement. What are some formative activities I might assign?"

When I put that prompt into Google's Bard, I get a range of fun options to choose from without providing anything but the general topic (Figure 5.14).

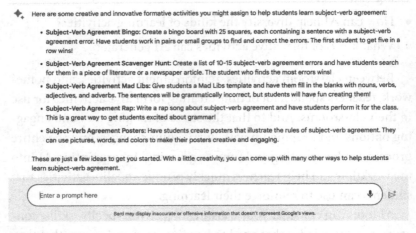

Here are some creative and innovative formative activities you might assign to help students learn subject-verb agreement:

- **Subject-Verb Agreement Bingo:** Create a bingo board with 25 squares, each containing a sentence with a subject-verb agreement error. Have students work in pairs or small groups to find and correct the errors. The first student to get five in a row wins!
- **Subject-Verb Agreement Scavenger Hunt:** Create a list of 10-15 subject-verb agreement errors and have students search for them in a piece of literature or a newspaper article. The student who finds the most errors wins!
- **Subject-Verb Agreement Mad Libs:** Give students a Mad Libs template and have them fill in the blanks with nouns, verbs, adjectives, and adverbs. The sentences will be grammatically incorrect, but students will have fun creating them!
- **Subject-Verb Agreement Rap:** Write a rap song about subject-verb agreement and have students perform it for the class. This is a great way to get students excited about grammar!
- **Subject-Verb Agreement Posters:** Have students create posters that illustrate the rules of subject-verb agreement. They can use pictures, words, and colors to make their posters creative and engaging.

These are just a few ideas to get you started. With a little creativity, you can come up with many other ways to help students learn subject-verb agreement.

Enter a prompt here

Bard may display inaccurate or offensive information that doesn't represent Google's views.

Figure 5.14 Google Bard output with multiple suggestions for formative activities that help students about subject-verb agreement.

Follow-Up

I can then follow up so that it makes the actual activity.

Prompt: "Can you draft the Mad Libs?"

Not only did Bard create a Mad Lib activity, but it also provided a sample answer key for what the correct answers might be (Figure 5.15).

There are various types of activities that you can ask AI tools to make for you. The following list has a range of options to get you started on most of these:

- **Quiz Creation:** AI tools can generate multiple-choice, true/false, fill-in-the-blank, and short-answer quizzes based on the provided subject/topic.

- **Essay Prompts:** AI tools can develop creative, analytical, persuasive, or narrative essay prompts.

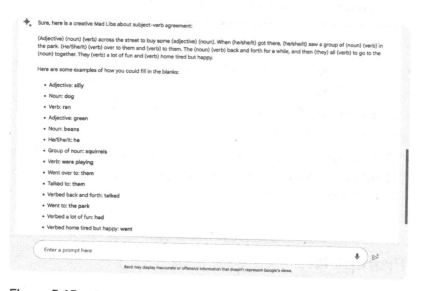

Figure 5.15   Google Bard output with sentences that have blanks for various parts of speech and a list of possible words for each blank.

- **Discussion Questions:** AI tools can help generate thought-provoking questions about a specific topic or lesson.

- **Writing Exercises:** AI can draft writing prompts to improve different aspects of writing, such as creativity, clarity, grammar, and vocabulary.

- **Problem Sets:** For subjects like math, physics, or computer science, AI tools can generate problem sets for practice and comprehension.

- **Role-Play Scenarios:** AI can create scenarios for role-play activities or simulations.

- **Project Ideas:** AI can provide suggestions for group or individual projects, including art projects, science experiments, history presentations, and more.

- **Reading Comprehension Questions:** After being provided an article or the content, AI tools can generate comprehension questions to check students' understanding of the material.

- **Research Topics:** AI tools can provide ideas for research papers or projects, and guiding questions to help students start their research.

- **Study Guides:** AI can create outlines or guides for studying a topic or preparing for a test.

- **Case Studies:** AI can draft a mock case study to help students think about a historical event or concept in social studies through examples and narrative.

Prompt It!

- **Multiple-Choice Questions:** "Generate a set of 10 multiple-choice questions on the water cycle for a 5th-grade science class."

- **Short Story:** "Create a short story illustrating the concept of photosynthesis for 4th graders."

- **Crossword Puzzle:** "Design a crossword puzzle on the key terminologies used in the American Revolutionary War for an 8th-grade history class."

- **Dialogue:** "Create a dialogue between two characters discussing the differences between plant and animal cells."

- **Fill-in-the-Blank Exercise:** "Design a fill-in-the-blank exercise on Shakespeare's *Romeo and Juliet* focusing on character analysis."

- **True or False Questions:** "Generate a set of true or false questions on the principles of economics for a high school economics class."

- **Persuasive Essay Prompt:** "Write a persuasive essay prompt on the importance of renewable energy sources for a high school English class."

- **Reading Comprehension:** "Create a reading comprehension passage and corresponding questions on the life of Isaac Newton for a 6th-grade science class."

- **Word Search Puzzle:** "Design a word search puzzle on vocabulary words related to geometry for a 7th-grade math class."

- **Jigsaw Reading:** "Create a jigsaw reading task on climate change for a 10th-grade environmental science class."

- **Role-Play Script:** "Generate a role-play script illustrating the concept of supply and demand for a high school economics class."

- **Worksheet:** "Generate a worksheet on balancing chemical equations for a 10th-grade chemistry class."

- **Matching Exercises:** "Design a set of matching exercises to learn the capitals of European countries for a 7th-grade geography class."

SUMMATIVE ASSESSMENTS: QUIZZES, RUBRICS, AND PERFORMANCE TASKS

- How can AI support the development of meaningful and authentic summative assessments?

- How can AI assist in creating rubrics and performance tasks that align with learning objectives?

- How can AI help teachers streamline grading and feedback processes?

Like the capabilities and benefits of using AI for formative activities, AI tools can help generate innovative assessments that are aligned with standards, targeted to the exact concepts and skills being tested, personalized to the needs of your classroom or individual students, and adapted to different teaching and learning goals. Some types of assessments that AI tools can help generate include:

- **Essay prompts:** AI tools can generate a variety of essay prompts for history, literature, social studies, and more.

- **Project ideas:** AI tools can generate ideas for long-term projects like science experiments, literature reviews, or community service projects.

- **Assessment questions:** AI tools can help create multiple-choice, true/false, short-answer, and essay questions for various topics.

- **Case studies:** For subjects like social studies, economics, or business studies, AI tools can design case studies for students to analyze.

- **Research topics:** AI tools can generate a list of potential research topics for students in various subjects.

- **Oral presentation topics:** AI tools can create a list of topics for students to prepare oral presentations.

- **Debate topics:** AI tools can generate interesting and challenging debate topics for language and social sciences.

- **Book report guidelines:** For literature or reading classes, AI tools can outline guidelines for book reports.

- **Simulation scenarios:** In science or social studies, AI tools can propose simulation scenarios for understanding complex concepts.

- **Portfolio creation guide:** For creative subjects, AI tools can outline steps and guidelines to create a portfolio showcasing students' work.

You can also ask it to take existing assessments and convert them into different types of assessments.

Conversion

Prompt: "Can you take this essay prompt and make it into a more interactive, problem-based assessment:

> 'Discuss the causes and effects of World War II, analyzing the significant factors that led to the outbreak of the war and the far-reaching consequences it had on global politics, economies, and societies.'"

ChatGPT came up with a fun, interactive, problem-based assessment to replace the essay prompt (Figure 5.16). In addition, similar

Problem-based Assessment: "Investigating the Legacy of World War II"

Introduction:
Welcome to "Investigating the Legacy of World War II"! In this interactive assessment, you will dive into the causes and effects of World War II. Your task is to analyze the significant factors that led to the outbreak of the war and the far-reaching consequences it had on global politics, economies, and societies. You will act as a historian and investigator, examining various sources and engaging in critical thinking to solve the mysteries surrounding this pivotal moment in history.

Task 1: Identify the Causes
Your first task is to identify the key causes of World War II. Explore primary sources, such as historical documents, speeches, photographs, and video footage, to uncover the factors that contributed to the outbreak of the war. As you gather evidence, consider the political, economic, and social factors that played a significant role. Compile your findings and present a comprehensive analysis of the causes, highlighting their interconnections and the impact they had on global relations.

Task 2: Investigate a Historical Event
For this task, you will investigate a specific historical event related to World War II. Choose an event that interests you, such as the invasion of Poland, the bombing of Pearl Harbor, or the Battle of Stalingrad. Utilize a variety of resources, including eyewitness accounts, historical narratives, and scholarly articles, to delve into the details of the event. Examine its causes, key players involved, strategies employed, and its consequences on both the military and civilian populations. Present your findings in an engaging manner, such as through a multimedia presentation or an interactive timeline.

Task 3: Analyze Far-Reaching Consequences
Now it's time to explore the far-reaching consequences of World War II on global politics, economies, and societies. Investigate how the war reshaped the geopolitical landscape, led to the formation of new alliances, and transformed power dynamics between nations. Consider the economic impact, such as the emergence of new economic systems and the reconstruction efforts that followed the war. Additionally, analyze the social and cultural effects, including the changes in gender roles, advancements in technology, and the establishment of international organizations. Prepare a reflective essay or a thought-provoking discussion on the lasting consequences of World War II.

Task 4: Evaluate Counterfactual Scenarios
In this final task, you will engage in critical thinking and evaluate counterfactual scenarios regarding World War II. Select one major event or decision during the war and speculate on an alternative outcome. How might the world have been different if that event or decision had unfolded differently? Analyze the potential impact on global politics, economies, and societies. Present your assessment through a creative format, such as a fictional story, an alternative history timeline, or a persuasive argument.

Conclusion:
Congratulations on completing the "Investigating the Legacy of World War II" assessment! Through your investigations, you have explored the causes and effects of World War II, delving into the significant factors that led to the outbreak of the war and the far-reaching consequences it had on global politics, economies, and societies. Your critical thinking and analysis have shed light on this transformative period in history, helping us better understand its enduring impact.

Figure 5.16   ChatGPT output with a broken-down problem-based assessment.

prompts from Chapter 4 can be combined with existing assessments to help convert them to align with different teaching strategies.

AI tools can also create rubrics and learning objectives for your assessments. The tools can help you create detailed and clear rubrics that align with learning standards and effectively test mastery of key concepts and skills. They can assist in creating rubrics by suggesting various criteria that could be used to assess students' understanding of a topic. For example, for an essay on the Civil War, AI tools might suggest criteria like "Accuracy of historical facts," "Clarity of argument," and "Use of evidence to support claims." It can also indicate various performance levels for each criterion, from "exceeds expectations" to "does not meet expectations."

Based on a given topic or subject area, AI tools can suggest various learning objectives that might be appropriate. For example, if you are teaching a unit on the American Civil War in a history class, it could offer learning objectives such as "Students will be able to explain the major causes of the Civil War" or "Students will be able to identify key figures and their roles during the Civil War."

AI tools can suggest performance tasks that align with the learning objectives. For example, for the objective "Students will be able to explain the major causes of the Civil War," it could suggest a task like "Write a short essay explaining the major causes of the Civil War, using evidence from primary and secondary sources to support your argument."

Taking the preceding example, we can ask it to create a rubric to help us evaluate this more complicated assessment.

Rubric

Prompt: "Can you make a rubric to grade this assessment and provide it in table format?"

ChatGPT took the assessment it made for us in the preceding prompt and generated a detailed rubric to evaluate student performance (Figure 5.17).

Criteria	Excellent (4)	Good (3)	Fair (2)	Poor (1)
Task 1: Identify the Causes	- Thoroughly identifies and analyzes the key causes of World War II with strong supporting evidence from a variety of relevant sources.	- Identifies and analyzes the key causes of World War II with sufficient supporting evidence from relevant sources.	- Identifies and analyzes some causes of World War II, but lacks depth or supporting evidence from relevant sources.	- Provides a limited or inaccurate analysis of the causes of World War II, with insufficient supporting evidence from relevant sources.
Task 2: Investigate a Historical Event	- Demonstrates a comprehensive investigation of a specific historical event related to World War II, showcasing a deep understanding of its causes, key players, strategies employed, and consequences. Presents findings in an engaging and creative manner.	- Conducts a solid investigation of a specific historical event related to World War II, providing a good understanding of its causes, key players, strategies employed, and consequences. Presents findings in a clear and organized manner.	- Conducts a basic investigation of a specific historical event related to World War II, but lacks depth in understanding its causes, key players, strategies employed, or consequences. Presents findings with limited organization or creativity.	- Provides a limited or inaccurate investigation of a historical event related to World War II, with little understanding of its causes, key players, strategies employed, or consequences. Presents findings in a disorganized or unclear manner.
Task 3: Analyze Far-Reaching Consequences	- Provides a comprehensive analysis of the far-reaching consequences of World War II on global politics, economies, and societies. Offers nuanced insights and demonstrates a deep understanding of the topic. Presents findings in a well-structured and thought-provoking manner.	- Provides a solid analysis of the far-reaching consequences of World War II on global politics, economies, and societies. Offers good insights and demonstrates a good understanding of the topic. Presents findings in a clear and organized manner.	- Provides a basic analysis of the far-reaching consequences of World War II, but lacks depth or significant insights. Presents findings with limited structure or thoughtfulness.	- Provides a limited or inaccurate analysis of the far-reaching consequences of World War II, with little understanding of the topic. Presents findings in a disorganized or unclear manner.

↻ Regenerate response

Figure 5.17 ChatGPT output with a rubric that grades the problem-based assignment from Figure 5.16.

Task 4: Evaluate Counterfactual Scenarios	- Engages in critical thinking and evaluates counterfactual scenarios with exceptional insight and creativity. Presents a well-reasoned and compelling argument, backed by evidence and analysis.	- Engages in critical thinking and evaluates counterfactual scenarios with good insight and creativity. Presents a well-reasoned argument supported by evidence and analysis.	- Engages in basic critical thinking and evaluates counterfactual scenarios, but lacks depth or creativity. Presents an argument with limited reasoning, evidence, or analysis.	- Provides a limited or inaccurate evaluation of counterfactual scenarios, with little critical thinking, creativity, or reasoning. Presents an argument with minimal evidence or analysis.
Overall Presentation and Communication of Findings	- Demonstrates exceptional organization, clarity, and creativity in presenting findings. Engages the audience effectively through an engaging and interactive format. Utilizes appropriate sources and demonstrates strong communication skills.	- Presents findings in a clear and organized manner. Effectively communicates the information using a suitable format. Uses relevant sources and demonstrates good communication skills.	- Presents findings with some organization and clarity, but lacks consistent structure or creativity. Communicates the information adequately using an acceptable format. Uses some relevant sources and demonstrates satisfactory communication skills.	- Presents findings with limited organization or clarity. Fails to effectively communicate the information using an appropriate format. Uses insufficient or irrelevant sources and demonstrates weak communication skills.
Critical Thinking and Analysis	- Demonstrates exceptional critical thinking skills throughout the assessment, offering insightful analysis, strong reasoning, and evidence-based conclusions. Shows a high level of intellectual curiosity and originality in approaching the tasks.	- Demonstrates good critical thinking skills throughout the assessment, providing solid analysis, reasoning, and evidence-based conclusions. Shows a satisfactory level of intellectual curiosity in approaching the tasks.	- Demonstrates basic critical thinking skills in the assessment, but lacks depth or strong reasoning. Presents some analysis and conclusions but with limited evidence.	- Provides limited or inaccurate critical thinking skills in the assessment, with little analysis, weak reasoning, or unsupported conclusions. Lacks intellectual curiosity in approaching the tasks.

Figure 5.17 *(Continued)*

These tools can also help with the feedback and grading step by helping you give proper feedback that is clear and productive. Of course, it can create answer keys to existing or new assessments to make it easier for you to grade, but it can also take your feedback and reword it, add more forward-looking steps, and ensure that it is fair and balanced across different students.

By cross-checking assessments and your grading, AI tools can help identify and mitigate potential biases in assessment design and grading, contributing to more reliable and valid assessment results. We discuss automated grading and feedback in the following chapter, but for now, you can think of AI tools as a second pair of eyes on your work!

Prompt It!

GENERATING SUMMATIVE ASSESSMENTS

- **Traditional:** "Create a summative assessment for a high school physics unit on mechanics, including multiple-choice, short-answer, and essay questions."

- **Project:** "Design an end-of-unit project for a middle school English class studying Shakespeare's *Romeo and Juliet*."

- **Exam:** "Generate a comprehensive exam for a college-level introductory biology course, focusing on cell biology and genetics."

- **Portfolio:** "Develop a portfolio-based assessment for a high school art class, detailing what pieces should be included and how they should be presented."

- **Scenarios:** "Create a scenario-based evaluation for a business management course, focusing on problem-solving and decision-making skills."

- **Evaluation Questions:** "Create an assessment for a history class focusing on World War II, including both factual recall and critical thinking questions."

- **Capstone:** "Design an end-of-course evaluation for a coding class where students must demonstrate their ability to create a simple app."

CREATING RUBRICS AND ALIGNING PERFORMANCE TASKS

- **Project Rubric:** "Create a detailed rubric for a middle school science fair project."

- **Performance Task:** "Design a performance task for a unit on the Civil Rights Movement in a high school history class, with a corresponding rubric for grading."

- **Group Work Rubric:** "Generate a rubric to evaluate group work in a college-level sociology class."

- **Essay Rubric:** "Generate a rubric for evaluating an essay in a college-level English Literature course."

- **Performance Task and Rubric:** "Design a performance task for a high school biology class on evolution, with an aligned rubric."

- **Specific Rubric:** "Create a rubric for a public speaking assignment, focusing on clarity, delivery, content, and audience engagement."

IMPLICATIONS FOR SPECIAL EDUCATION, ELL, AND INCLUSIVE CLASSROOMS

- What are the benefits of AI for inclusive classrooms?
- How can AI be used to support students with special needs?
- How can AI-generated resources help ELLs?

The personalized learning possible with AI has been discussed in earlier sections and chapters and is covered deeper in Chapter 7. All of the ways in which AI can be used to differentiate learning and personalize instruction can help teachers create a more inclusive classroom. AI tools can serve as effective teaching assistants and learning buddies to ensure that the students who need personal attention receive it. The ability for students to gain immediate feedback and support and to collect and analyze data quickly to spot learning gaps and patterns all make the future of education more inclusive. At the same time, these systems will need to be specially crafted and monitored to ensure that they reduce biases and discrepancies rather than perpetuate them.

In the section on differentiation in Chapter 4, we discuss the various ways teachers can use AI tools to differentiate content. The automatic generation of alternative learning materials and formats will help meet more students where they are.

This includes creating learning resources that apply Universal Design for Learning principles (UDL), providing alternative modalities of materials (text-to-speech), and adapting material for different student needs (i.e., changing the cultural context of a reading comprehension passage to avoid bias). This also includes ensuring diverse representation in educational materials, whether that is the graphics on presentation slides, contexts for math word problems, or how information is presented and taught.

AI tools can also be used to evaluate existing materials to ensure they are accessible and then adapt them to reduce any accessibility challenges that are present in them. They can also do things such as adjusting font size, color contrast, or audio speed. As AI tools continue to grow in education, the integration of assistive technologies will be a critical piece of ensuring that our classrooms become more inclusive, not less.

As the AI tools become better integrated with existing tools, teachers will have more robust data about where students are falling behind, what interventions are likely to support struggling students, and the longer-term trends in a student's performance and needs. In addition, chatbots will likely be available for socioemotional support and executive functioning development.

Teachers in special education will be able to modify the differentiation prompts to be even more specific to the needs of their students to ensure that the content adaptation and creation align with their needs. For example, AI might adapt content to a particular Flesch-Kincaid Level to ensure student comprehension. AI can also be used to scaffold activities for struggling students further. For example, teachers can feed assessments to the AI tools and ask for a detailed step-by-step breakdown for students to complete the activity. Teachers can also use tools to generate IEPs (Individualized Education Programs), implement specific modifications or accommodations in their material, or ask for suggestions on changes they can make based on a particular IEP.

Teachers who teach English language learners can also use AI tools to assist their students better. For example, they can have AI tools translate back and forth much more easily to communicate clearly with their students. They can also use language scaffolding and have AI tools create immersive exercises that integrate the student's native language with English to build fluency slowly. They can also allow the student to complete assignments in non-language classes in their native language and then have AI tools with capabilities in that language to evaluate the work.

AI tools are also available that directly target language learning. These tools help students by correcting pronunciation, gamifying language learning, and providing natural, immersive conversation opportunities. For example, teachers can assign dialogues on Socrat. ai to have students role-play and practice using English in real-life scenarios, and it can help students practice concepts until they develop mastery.

The potential for AI to make our classrooms and schools more inclusive for all learners, including those with learning needs and ELL, is one of the tremendous benefits of integrating AI. In addition, the increase in personalized learning, improved communication, real-time feedback, and data-driven insights will all enable us to serve our students better.

Prompt It!

SPECIAL EDUCATION:

- **Scaffold:** "Generate a step-by-step guide for teaching basic arithmetic to students with learning disabilities."

- **Tailored Activities:** "Create a list of sensory activities suitable for children with autism in a classroom setting."

- **Differentiated Prompts:** "Propose a set of creative writing prompts for students with dyslexia."

- **Visual Learning:** "Generate a series of visual aids to help explain the concept of fractions to students with special needs."

- **IEP Goals:** "Help me draft IEP goals for a 5th-grade student with dyslexia focusing on reading comprehension."

- **IEP Objectives:** "Suggest measurable objectives for an IEP for a student with ADHD focusing on improving attention and focus."

- **IEP Meetings:** "Given the following IEP {fill}, What kind of data should I gather to present at an IEP meeting?"

- **Brainstorm:** "What accommodations should be considered for a student with ADHD in a mainstream classroom?"

ELLs:

- **Lesson Plan:** "Design a lesson plan to teach basic English vocabulary through immersive activities."

- **Research:** "Create a list of storybooks suitable for beginner ELL students."

- **Prompts:** "Generate a set of conversation prompts to encourage ELL students to practice speaking English."

- **Scaffold:** "Create a step-by-step guide for writing a persuasive essay for advanced ELL students."

- **Flashcards:** "Create a series of flashcards for teaching English phrasal verbs."

- **Immersion:** "Write a short story using the student's native language and English."

- **Translation:** "Translate this essay from the student's native language to English for me to grade."

INCLUSIVE CLASSROOMS:

- **UDL:** "Make sure this lesson plan incorporates Universal Design for Learning (UDL) principles: {fill}."

- **Diversify Teaching:** "Design a lesson plan that incorporates multicultural perspectives in the study of history."

- **Cultural Exploration:** "Create a step-by-step guide for a project that allows students to explore their cultural heritage."

- **Resources:** "Generate a list of resources for inclusively teaching about different types of families."

- **Guidance:** "Create a guide on how to adapt a physical education class to be inclusive for students of all physical abilities."

DISTANCE AND REMOTE EDUCATION

- How can AI support effective remote instruction and distance learning?

- What are some practical ways to incorporate AI-powered tools into virtual classrooms?

Since the Covid-19 pandemic, schools have been more open to integrating distance and remote education, whether for summer school, electives, or as an emergency option during snow days. The digital environment of remote learning makes it the perfect place to heavily integrate AI technologies to continue to reduce educational barriers dependent on location. In addition, as large MOOCs (massive open online courses), global universities, and other educational institutions try to reach more students, they can take advantage of AI tools to create more robust digital experiences.

The amount of data produced through remote instruction (from discussion forums, recorded lectures and group discussions, chats, and online assessments) allows us to use AI's capabilities to improve learning. For example, AI systems could track how much a student speaks during a class and what they say, give the instructor insight into what concepts students struggled with the most, and it could adapt a pre-recorded lecture for each student based on their preferences.

AI could also be an additional instructor by offering personalized, on-demand tutoring and support for students and supplementing either in-person or remote instruction. For example, it could answer questions that students have mid-lecture or provide one-on-one support at any hour. Online classes could also incorporate intelligent discussion forums with AI-powered bots to facilitate knowledge sharing and collaboration among students by asking questions, following up on questions, and making connections between different posts that students make.

In addition, with asynchronous remote learning, it would be easier for instructors to offer individualized learning paths, where AI creates tailored learning paths that adapt to each student's needs, abilities, and goals. More on these are covered in Chapter 7.

By leveraging AI technology in distance and remote education, educators can create more engaging, personalized, and effective learning experiences for students, transcending the limitations of physical classrooms.

Prompt It!

- **Lesson Planning:** "Design a comprehensive lesson plan for a sixth grade distance education class focusing on the water cycle. The lesson should be engaging, include interactive elements, and conclude with a short quiz."

- **Time Management:** "Generate a list of best practices for students to effectively manage their time while learning from home in a distance education model."

- **Asynchronous Curriculum Design:** "Design an interactive, self-paced module for teaching algebra to high school students in a distance learning environment. Include visual aids, step-by-step instructions, and practice problems."

- **Teacher Coaching:** "Create a step-by-step guide on effectively using breakout rooms in a virtual classroom to foster group discussions and collaborative learning."

- **Icebreaker:** "Design an engaging virtual classroom icebreaker activity for the first day of school that fosters community and helps students get to know each other."

- **Incorporate VR:** "Generate a lesson plan incorporating virtual reality (VR) technology to teach a high school biology class about the human circulatory system."

- **Digital Scavenger Hunt:** "Design an interactive digital scavenger hunt activity for middle school students studying world geography in a remote learning setting."

CONCLUSION

This chapter outlines many ways for teachers to incorporate AI tools into their classrooms to streamline their workflow for curriculum management. The wide range of capabilities that AI technology has makes the possibilities for utilization by teachers just as broad.

The chapter also illustrates the crucial role that teachers will continue to play in classrooms as they prompt, iterate, and vet all the content created by AI systems, and ultimately interface directly with students during direct instruction. While AI can significantly aid in creating and revising educational materials, it cannot replicate the nuanced understanding, empathy, and interpersonal connection a human teacher brings to the classroom. Therefore, it should be seen as a tool to assist teachers, not replace them.

Throughout this chapter, we explored the promising potential of AI in curriculum development and developed a clear understanding of how to thoughtfully and effectively incorporate AI tools into your teaching practices.

Exit Ticket

Choose one unit from your curriculum and use an AI tool of your choice and your favorite prompts from this chapter to develop brand-new lesson plans, formative activities, and assessments. Try to use some of the learning theories from Chapter 4 when appropriate. Make sure you edit and check the material for any mistakes or inaccuracies before actually using them!

Chapter 6

Automating Administrative Tasks

Recent AI developments promise opportunities for increased efficiency, personalized support, and enhanced communication. In addition, through various tools and generative AI bots, education has the potential to reshape logistics significantly.

AI can improve communication among educators, students, and parents. With the ability to generate updates on student progress and manage messages, AI ensures timely and efficient communication. Virtual assistants can provide accurate information, answer common questions, and facilitate multilingual communication. AI can also send automated reminders for important events or deadlines and use sentiment analysis to provide insights into the effectiveness of communication strategies.

AI has the potential to take over grading, which has traditionally been tedious and time-consuming, by automating grading and offering consistent, objective feedback to students. This shift promises to free up time for educators, allowing them to focus more on teaching and forging meaningful connections with their students.

For classroom organization and efficiency, AI can optimize class operations and reduce conflicts through intelligent scheduling and automatic organization of digital resources. In addition, it can simplify classroom management by automating routine tasks.

The potential for AI in education is vast, and we are only just beginning to tap into it. As we navigate this exciting era, the key is to embrace the possibilities, adapt to the changes, and use the potential benefits whenever possible.

STREAMLINING COMMUNICATION AND SCHEDULING

- How can AI support clear and effective communication among students, teachers, and parents?

- How can AI-powered chatbots and virtual assistants help manage classroom communications?

Teachers need to communicate daily with each other, their students, the students' parents, and administrators. All of this adds up to a significant chunk of the workload being communication. AI tools can take over a lot of communication and make it easier for teachers to handle communication in less time.

AI might even make the amount of communication between teachers and parents even better. For example, AI could generate personalized messages for every parent, synthesize feedback on recent assignments, including missing assignments from the grade book, and remind parents of events relevant to their child. The news could also be translated in real-time for parents for whom English isn't a first language.

AI could also streamline incoming communication by synthesizing information a teacher is receiving, analyzing the sentiments of emails from parents to determine what their emotions are, and auto-responding to emails to which it has the answers. It can also schedule meetings based on the teacher's calendar, reach out when a parent hasn't been heard from in a while, and remind the teacher about emails they must respond to directly with a draft response prepared.

AI bots that listen to meetings (either in-person or virtual) can also draft action items, suggest follow-up communication, and prepare personalized reports and talking points for the teacher before any other meetings. They could also directly answer questions that parents and students might have in natural language formats, similar to online chatbots, based on grade books, syllabi, and the school handbook.

This sounds like a utopian world, but every single step is already possible with existing technology.

While these technologies are being further integrated into classrooms, teachers can use existing tools to help them with communication needs.

Student Email

Prompt: "Draft an email to a student who keeps turning in late work, reminding them that my late policy is they have 48 hours to submit assignments for half points. Provide some constructive next steps."

ChatGPT is able to draft a comprehensive email that reminds the student of the policy, provides concrete next steps, and is empathetic. (See Figure 6.1.) ChatGPT's response will not waiver based on patience levels, time of day, or how many late notices it has already sent out!

Subject: Important Notice: Consistent Timeliness for Assignments and Late Submission Policy Reminder

Dear [Student's Name],

I hope this message finds you well.

I am writing to address an issue that has come to my attention regarding the timely submission of your coursework. I have noticed that several of your assignments have been handed in past their respective due dates, which is impacting your overall grade.

I understand that balancing multiple responsibilities can sometimes be challenging, and unexpected issues can arise that may interfere with your ability to meet deadlines. However, consistent adherence to assignment due dates is a crucial part of maintaining your academic performance.

As a reminder, per the syllabus and classroom guidelines, we do have a late submission policy in place which allows students a grace period of 48 hours after the due date to submit late assignments. However, please note that these assignments are only eligible for a maximum of half of the total points.

While this policy is designed to offer some flexibility in extreme circumstances, it's important to remember that habitual late submissions can significantly lower your overall grade.

Here are a few suggestions on how to improve your time management skills and adhere to deadlines:

1. **Planning and Prioritization**: Use a planner or digital calendar to track assignment due dates. Prioritize tasks based on their due dates and the effort needed to complete them.
2. **Set Reminders**: Consider setting reminders a few days before the assignment is due to ensure you have ample time to complete it.
3. **Ask for Help Early**: If you're struggling with an assignment, don't hesitate to ask for assistance ahead of time. I am here to support your learning process, and early communication can allow us to find a solution together.
4. **Create a Routine**: Establish a consistent study routine to manage your workload effectively. This routine can help ensure you are dedicating sufficient time to your assignments.

I am confident that you are fully capable of turning this situation around, and I would be more than happy to meet during office hours or set up a separate time to discuss any concerns or challenges you may be experiencing. Your success in this class is my priority, and I am here to support you in any way I can.

Please remember that the key to success in any field is to manage your time effectively, and adhering to deadlines is a crucial part of that process. I believe in your abilities and am certain that with a bit of organization and planning, you can overcome this hurdle.

Thank you for your attention to this matter. I look forward to seeing your timely submissions in the future.

Figure 6.1   ChatGPT output of an email to a student with detailed steps.

Syllabus Component

Prompt: "I'm working on the syllabus for my high school science class, and I want to address the use of AI through a policy. I want students to use AI as a resource and tool and submit all original work."

Again, as seen in Figure 6.2, based on very little information, Bard creates a detailed policy for students with clarity, justifications, and a reminder about reaching out for more information.

Administrator Request

Prompt: "I'm drafting a letter to my principal to let me use Socrat.ai, a custom chatbot, to assign a Socratic dialogue to my students."

As seen in Figure 6.3, ChatGPT formats the letter correctly, includes a well-formed argument, and makes assumptions about what the tool does and what the school might be concerned about that are logical.

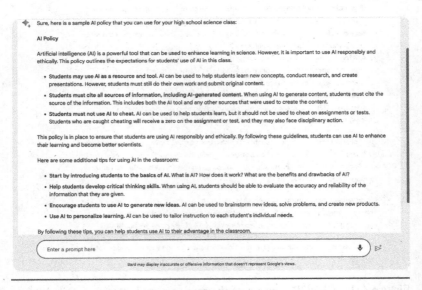

Figure 6.2 Google Bard output of a detailed policy for students on AI use.

[Your Name]
[Your Address]
[City, State, ZIP]
[Email Address]
[Phone Number]
[Date]

[Principal's Name]
[Principal's Designation]
[School Name]
[School Address]
[City, State, ZIP]

Subject: Request for Permission to Use Socrat.ai for Socratic Dialogues in the Classroom

Dear [Principal's Name],

I hope this letter finds you well. I am writing to request your permission to incorporate Socrat.ai, a custom chat bot, as a teaching tool in my classroom. I believe that this innovative technology will greatly enhance the learning experience and foster critical thinking skills among my students.

As an educator committed to providing quality education, I am always on the lookout for innovative tools that can engage and challenge my students. After thorough research and consideration, I have come across Socrat.ai, an advanced chat bot specifically designed to facilitate Socratic dialogues. This tool offers a unique and interactive way for students to engage in meaningful discussions, analyze concepts, and develop their critical thinking abilities.

Socrat.ai is equipped with powerful natural language processing capabilities, allowing it to engage in dynamic conversations with students. It can simulate a Socratic dialogue by posing thoughtful questions, providing prompts for further analysis, and encouraging students to explore different perspectives. By leveraging artificial intelligence, Socrat.ai adapts to individual student needs, ensuring a personalized learning experience for each student.

I firmly believe that integrating Socrat.ai into my teaching methodology will yield numerous benefits. Some key advantages include:

Figure 6.3 ChatGPT output with a fully formatted letter written to the principal.

1. Enhanced Critical Thinking: Socrat.ai will foster critical thinking skills by encouraging students to delve deeper into subject matter, consider different viewpoints, and engage in reasoned discussions.
2. Increased Student Engagement: The interactive nature of Socrat.ai will captivate students' attention and actively involve them in the learning process, resulting in higher levels of engagement and participation.
3. Personalized Learning: Socrat.ai's adaptive capabilities will cater to individual students' needs, offering personalized prompts and guidance to help them grasp complex concepts at their own pace.
4. Efficient Assessment: The chat bot's ability to record and analyze student conversations will provide valuable insights for me as an educator. It will help me identify areas of strength and weakness, allowing me to tailor my instructional approach accordingly.
5. Preparation for Real-World Skills: Socratic dialogues are not only an academic exercise but also an invaluable preparation for students' future endeavors. By using Socrat.ai, students will develop effective communication skills, critical thinking abilities, and an open-mindedness to diverse perspectives.

I understand the importance of maintaining a safe and controlled environment for my students. Rest assured that I have thoroughly evaluated Socrat.ai and found it to be a secure and reliable educational tool. The platform complies with strict privacy and data protection regulations, ensuring the confidentiality and anonymity of student interactions.

I kindly request your permission to pilot the use of Socrat.ai in my classroom for the duration of [specific time period]. During this trial period, I will closely monitor its impact on student engagement and academic performance. I will also be readily available to address any concerns or questions that may arise from both students and parents.

I am confident that Socrat.ai will contribute significantly to the educational experience of my students, aligning with our school's commitment to fostering critical thinking and preparing them for success. I would be grateful if you could grant me permission to use this tool, and I am open to discussing any guidelines or conditions you deem necessary for its implementation.

Thank you for your time and consideration. I look forward to discussing this matter further and working together to provide the best possible education for our students.

Sincerely,

[Your Name]

Figure 6.3   *(Continued)*

Parent Response

Prompt: "I've received the following email from a parent: 'I am beyond outraged to learn that *To Kill a Mockingbird* is part of your curriculum. This book promotes violence against innocent creatures and normalizes injustice. As a parent, I demand an immediate removal of this appalling content from my child's education. Failure to comply will have severe consequences.' Can you draft a direct response that doesn't escalate the situation but succinctly defends my use of the book?"

As seen in Figure 6.4, ChatGPT provides a robust defense of the use of *To Kill a Mockingbird*, which is empathetic but still makes clear that the book will be continued to be taught.

Newsletter

Prompt: "I'm working on a monthly newsletter to parents for my 5th-grade classroom. Can you ask me some questions and then draft the newsletter?"

This is an important example because it highlights the ability of AI tools to help you figure out what information they need to complete the task for you. As seen in Figure 6.5, they're able to ask questions that you may need to answer for them to draft a relevant newsletter.

In most scenarios, teachers can feed in the communication they have received (with consideration for compliance with student privacy laws) and have ChatGPT draft a starting point for them to respond. The ability of the AI to remain objective and still project empathy through its use of language makes it an excellent tool for teachers to draft emails. Google's Bard lets users directly export the response to Gmail; other tools offer alternatives.

Subject: Regarding "To Kill a Mockingbird" in the Curriculum

Dear [Parent's Name],

I hope this email finds you well. I appreciate your concerns regarding the inclusion of "To Kill a Mockingbird" in our curriculum. As an educator, I understand and value the importance of open communication and addressing parental concerns.

Firstly, it's important to note that "To Kill a Mockingbird" is a renowned literary work that has been taught in classrooms across the country for several decades. Its inclusion in the curriculum stems from its powerful portrayal of social issues and its ability to spark meaningful discussions among students.

While I understand your perspective that the book promotes violence against innocent creatures, it's essential to consider the broader context and themes explored within the novel. "To Kill a Mockingbird" delves into themes of racial inequality, injustice, empathy, and the moral growth of its young protagonist. By exposing students to these complex topics, we aim to encourage critical thinking, foster empathy, and promote a deeper understanding of historical and social realities.

Moreover, it is crucial to recognize that literature often reflects the realities of the time in which it was written. "To Kill a Mockingbird" provides an opportunity for students to examine the historical context of racial tensions in the United States, fostering discussions on the progress we have made as a society and the work that remains.

I understand that as a parent, you have concerns about the content your child is exposed to, and I assure you that our curriculum selection process involves careful consideration and alignment with educational standards. However, I believe that exposure to a variety of perspectives through literature helps students develop critical thinking skills, empathy, and a broader worldview.

I would be more than willing to schedule a meeting with you to discuss your concerns further and explore alternative educational resources that may address your worries while still fulfilling the educational goals of our curriculum. Working together, we can ensure a positive learning environment for your child.

Thank you for bringing your concerns to my attention, and I look forward to further discussion.

Sincerely,

[Your Name]
[Your Title/Position]

Figure 6.4   ChatGPT output of a clearly written email response to the parent letter.

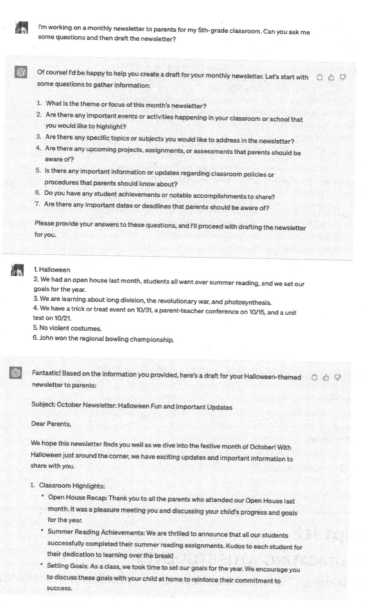

I'm working on a monthly newsletter to parents for my 5th-grade classroom. Can you ask me some questions and then draft the newsletter?

Of course! I'd be happy to help you create a draft for your monthly newsletter. Let's start with some questions to gather information:

1. What is the theme or focus of this month's newsletter?
2. Are there any important events or activities happening in your classroom or school that you would like to highlight?
3. Are there any specific topics or subjects you would like to address in the newsletter?
4. Are there any upcoming projects, assignments, or assessments that parents should be aware of?
5. Is there any important information or updates regarding classroom policies or procedures that parents should know about?
6. Do you have any student achievements or notable accomplishments to share?
7. Are there any important dates or deadlines that parents should be aware of?

Please provide your answers to these questions, and I'll proceed with drafting the newsletter for you.

1. Halloween
2. We had an open house last month, students all went over summer reading, and we set our goals for the year.
3. We are learning about long division, the revolutionary war, and photosynthesis.
4. We have a trick or treat event on 10/31, a parent-teacher conference on 10/15, and a unit test on 10/21.
5. No violent costumes.
6. John won the regional bowling championship.

Fantastic! Based on the information you provided, here's a draft for your Halloween-themed newsletter to parents:

Subject: October Newsletter: Halloween Fun and Important Updates

Dear Parents,

We hope this newsletter finds you well as we dive into the festive month of October! With Halloween just around the corner, we have exciting updates and important information to share with you.

1. Classroom Highlights:
   * Open House Recap: Thank you to all the parents who attended our Open House last month. It was a pleasure meeting you and discussing your child's progress and goals for the year.
   * Summer Reading Achievements: We are thrilled to announce that all our students successfully completed their summer reading assignments. Kudos to each student for their dedication to learning over the break!
   * Setting Goals: As a class, we took time to set our goals for the year. We encourage you to discuss these goals with your child at home to reinforce their commitment to success.

Figure 6.5   ChatGPT screenshot with initial prompt, output of questions from ChatGPT, responses from user, and the final newsletter content output.

2. Curriculum Focus:
   * Math: Currently, we are diving into the world of long division. Students are sharpening their division skills and practicing problem-solving strategies. Encourage your child to review division facts at home for extra practice.
   * Social Studies: We have embarked on an exciting journey through the Revolutionary War. Students are exploring the causes, major events, and influential figures that shaped this significant period in American history.
   * Science: Our science lessons are illuminating as we delve into the fascinating world of photosynthesis. Your child will learn about the process of converting light energy into chemical energy in plants. It's an excellent opportunity for hands-on experiments and discussions at home.
3. Upcoming Events:
   * Trick or Treat Event: On October 31st, we will be celebrating Halloween in the classroom. Students are encouraged to come dressed in their favorite costumes (please remember no violent costumes). We will have a fun-filled day of activities, games, and treats. Stay tuned for more details!
   * Parent-Teacher Conference: Our first parent-teacher conference of the year will take place on October 15th. This is an excellent opportunity for us to discuss your child's progress, address any concerns, and strengthen our partnership in supporting their education. We will be reaching out to schedule appointments soon.
   * Unit Test: Please mark your calendars for the unit test on October 21st. This assessment will gauge your child's understanding of the topics covered so far. Encourage them to review their notes and complete any assigned practice problems to prepare.
4. Celebrating Student Success:
   We are thrilled to announce that John, one of our talented students, recently won the regional bowling championship! Let's congratulate him on this remarkable achievement. It's wonderful to see our students excel outside the classroom.

We value your involvement and support in your child's education. If you have any questions, concerns, or would like to discuss anything further, please don't hesitate to reach out to us.

Wishing you a spooktacular Halloween filled with joy and memorable moments!

Best regards,

[Your Name]
[Your Email]
[Your Phone Number]

Figure 6.5   *(Continued)*

Prompt It!

COMMUNICATING WITH STUDENTS

- **Reminders:** "Draft a message to my students reminding them about the upcoming project due date, including details on the requirements and tips for success."

- **Feedback:** "Generate a personalized feedback message for a student who performed well on the recent test, praising their efforts and encouraging further learning."

- **Motivational Message:** "Help me construct a motivational message to send to my students struggling with the current topic."

- **Announcements:** "Create an announcement about an upcoming field trip, including details like date, time, location, and things to bring."

- **Policies:** "Compose a message explaining the change in the homework policy to my students. Make sure it's easy to understand and addresses potential questions."

COMMUNICATING WITH ADMIN

- **Request:** "Draft a request for additional resources for my classroom. Focus on the benefits for student learning."

- **Interest Letter:** "Compose a message to the school principal expressing my interest in leading a new extracurricular club."

- **Report:** "Ask me questions to help me generate a report summarizing the academic performance of my class this semester and highlighting both strengths and areas for improvement."

- **Proposal:** "Help me write a proposal for a professional development workshop I want to conduct for the teaching staff."

- **Email:** "Create an email informing the administrative staff about a maintenance issue in my classroom."

COMMUNICATING WITH PARENTS

- **Update:** "Compose a message to a parent regarding their child's excellent performance in the recent school project."

- **Reminder:** "Generate an email to parents about the importance of regular bedtime for their children's academic performance."

- **Careful Message:** "Draft a delicate message to a parent about their child's recent disruptive classroom behavior. Make sure to offer ways to work together to improve it."

- **Newsletter:** "Help me write a newsletter for parents outlining the upcoming events and important dates for the next month."

- **Explain:** "Construct an email to a parent who has requested more information about the reading materials used in class by explaining the choices and how they benefit their child's learning. Here's our reading list {fill}."

AI-ENHANCED FEEDBACK AND GRADING

- How can AI tools provide personalized feedback to students?
- How can AI improve the accuracy and consistency of grading?
- What are the challenges and limitations of using AI for grading and assessment?

While we have already discussed AI's ability to help teachers provide feedback, AI tools can go one step further and provide the feedback themselves. AI systems can break down rubrics, grading requirements, or assignment instructions and then grade assignments with feedback for students. The ability to quickly generate individual feedback for an infinite number of students is an appealing feature of incorporating AI tools into classrooms. The feedback would also be in real-time, allowing students to receive feedback much quicker than if a teacher had to review every student's work individually.

While AI tools are still being incorporated into classrooms, educators must also be careful about integrating them into the grading and feedback flow. For example, it would be important to ensure that the AI tools are provided with the learning objectives and any standards to ensure alignment between the grade, feedback, and actual goals of the assignments. Educators should also review the feedback and grades to ensure they align with their own judgment and accurately reflect the student's work.

While the thought of AI-graded assignments might seem frightening to some, the potential for AI to reduce bias and subjectivity in grading makes it a promising addition to the grading process. AI algorithms can analyze student work objectively and reduce the influence of personal biases on grading. The tools will still be customized to follow specific grading criteria to ensure the grades are consistent and further reduce subjectivity.

Essay Feedback

Prompt: "Provide constructive feedback to my 8th-grade student on this essay:

> Title: The Amazing World of Nutritian
> Nutrition is like, um, super important for our bodies and stuff. It's like the fuel that keeps us going, just like the gas in a car. We need to eat healthy foods to stay strong and be able to do all the things we want to do. But sometimes, it can be kinda hard to understand all this nutrition stuff. So, let's dive into the amazing world of nutrition together!

Firstly, there are different types of foods that we eat. There are the healthy foods like fruits, vegetables, whole grains, and lean proteins. These foods are like superheroes for our bodies because they give us lots of energy and help us grow big and strong. Then, there are the not-so-healthy foods like fast food, sugary snacks, and soda. These foods might taste good, but they don't really give us much nutrition and can make us feel yucky if we eat too much of them.

One of the most important things about nutrition is getting all the different nutrients that our bodies need. Nutrients are like the vitamins and minerals that make our bodies work properly. They help us stay healthy and fight off germs. Some of the important nutrients are vitamins A, C, and D, calcium, and iron. We can get these nutrients from eating a variety of healthy foods. It's like putting together a puzzle, where each piece is a different nutrient that our bodies need.

Another thing that's really important is drinking water. Water is like the superhero sidekick of nutrition. It helps us stay hydrated and keeps our bodies running smoothly. We should drink water every day and try to limit sugary drinks like soda and juice. Water is the best choice for quenching our thirst and keeping us healthy.

Eating a balanced diet is also a big part of nutrition. It's like having a mix of different foods on your plate. We should try to fill half of our plate with fruits and vegetables, a quarter with whole grains like brown rice or whole wheat bread, and a quarter with lean proteins like chicken or fish. This way, we're getting a little bit of everything we need to keep our bodies healthy and strong.

But hey, I get it, sometimes it's hard to eat healthy all the time. I mean, pizza and ice cream are just too good to resist sometimes! It's okay to have those foods once in a while as a treat, but we should try to make healthier choices most of the time. Maybe we can have a small slice of pizza and then fill the rest of our plate with a salad or some veggies.

In conclusion, nutrition is really important for our bodies. We need to eat healthy foods, drink water, and get all the nutrients we need to stay strong and healthy. It's not always easy, but by making small changes and trying our best, we can make a big difference in our health. So let's embrace the amazing world of nutrition and fuel our bodies with the goodness they deserve!"

ChatGPT provides clear, actionable feedback to the student that can be a starting place for the teacher's own work with the student (Figure 6.6).

The current risks of AI-led grading and feedback are not insignificant. AI tools may misinterpret complex or nuanced student responses and thus provide inaccurate grading or feedback. They may also not be able to take into account the context that the teacher has from their experience with the student or even classroom discussions. Concerns about privacy, data security, and potential biases in the existing AI systems must be addressed before AI tools can be fully trusted to decide grades unanimously.

For now, educators should adopt a balanced approach and use AI-generated feedback to supplement their expertise and observations. Thus, educators can ensure any grades or feedback aligns with their understanding of the student's progress. Teachers can also combine AI-generated feedback with their own comments to prevent leaving out anything that would help students learn from their work. While these technologies remain new to the classroom environment, educators should reflect on their use of AI-generated feedback and evaluate its impact on student learning and their own teaching practice on an ongoing basis.

Overall, your essay provides a good introduction to the topic of nutrition and presents some key ideas effectively. However, there are areas where you can improve your writing to make it more clear and concise. Here are some constructive feedback points:

1. Clarity and Organization:

* Try to use more precise and specific language throughout the essay. Avoid vague terms like "um" and "stuff" and use clear and concise sentences to convey your ideas.
* Consider organizing your essay into paragraphs to make it easier to read and follow. Each paragraph can focus on a specific aspect of nutrition, such as types of foods, nutrients, water, and balanced diet.

2. Tone and Language:

* Maintain a consistent tone throughout the essay. While it's great to use a conversational style, make sure it remains appropriate for an academic essay. Avoid slang and colloquial language.
* Make use of transitional words and phrases to improve the flow and coherence of your essay. This will help connect your ideas more smoothly.

3. Expansion of Ideas:

* Expand on the importance of healthy foods by providing examples of specific fruits, vegetables, whole grains, and lean proteins. This will make your essay more informative and engaging for the reader.
* Elaborate on the role of nutrients by explaining how each of the mentioned vitamins and minerals contributes to our overall health. Consider providing examples of foods rich in these nutrients.
* Discuss the benefits of drinking water in more detail. Explain why it's important for hydration, as well as for digestion, circulation, and overall bodily functions.
* When discussing a balanced diet, you can provide more specific examples of different foods that fall into each category (fruits and vegetables, whole grains, and lean proteins).

4. Addressing Challenges:

* While acknowledging the difficulty of maintaining a healthy diet, provide some strategies or tips for making healthier choices on a regular basis. Offer practical suggestions for incorporating healthy foods into daily meals and snacks.

By implementing these suggestions, you can enhance the clarity, organization, and depth of your essay. Remember to revise and proofread your work to ensure correct grammar, punctuation, and spelling. Keep up the good work!

Figure 6.6 ChatGPT output of essay feedback with clear areas of improvement for the student.

Prompt It!

GRADING AND PROVIDING FEEDBACK

- **Detailed Feedback:** "Provide detailed feedback on a student's essay on the causes of the American Revolution based on these instructions {fill}."

- **Constructive Feedback:** "Grade and offer constructive feedback on a high school student's science lab report {fill}."

- **Specific Feedback:** "Provide feedback on a student's coding project. Focus on code readability, efficiency, and correctness."

- **Apply Rubric:** "Apply the following rubric to this response and provide a score in each category {fill}."

OPTIMIZING PAPERWORK AND RECORDKEEPING TASKS

- What are the key features of AI tools for paperwork and record-keeping tasks?

- How can AI tools simplify the management of student records and documentation?

Our education system runs on a lot of paperwork and recordkeeping. A lot of recordkeeping is involved, whether it be student work, grades, feedback or teacher evaluations, HR files, and performance-improvement plans!

Some of the benefits of integrating AI into our recordkeeping include:

- **Advanced search capabilities:** AI tools can employ advanced search functions and make locating specific documents or information easier.

- **Text recognition:** AI tools can utilize Optical Character Recognition (OCR) technology to digitize and categorize handwritten or printed documents.

- **Summarizing:** AI tools can analyze and extract relevant information from text documents to make it quicker for teachers to act on the stored information.

- **Data analysis:** AI tools can analyze student records to identify patterns and trends and provide valuable insights for educators and administrators.

AI tools can also help create templates, forms, and other paperwork necessary for the daily operations of our schools.

Permission Slip

Prompt: "Generate a permission slip for a field trip to the Natural History Museum with the relevant information for parents, disclosures, and placeholders for my contact information. We'll be there all day on March 1, take the school bus, and everyone has to bring bagged lunch. We also need two parent chaperones."

The permission slip is formatted correctly, has placeholders for information the teacher needs to provide, and has outlined all the important information (Figure 6.7).

While the paperwork and recordkeeping are important in ensuring safety for our students in many ways, offloading the work

[Your School Logo]

Permission Slip: Field Trip to the Natural History Museum

Dear Parent/Guardian,

We are excited to announce a field trip to the Natural History Museum on March 1st. This trip will provide a valuable educational experience for our students, allowing them to explore the wonders of nature, science, and history. We kindly request your permission for your child to participate in this field trip.

Trip Details:

* Destination: Natural History Museum
* Date: March 1st
* Duration: All day
* Mode of Transportation: School Bus
* Lunch: Students are required to bring a bagged lunch

Disclosures:

1. Safety: The Natural History Museum is committed to ensuring the safety of all visitors. The museum follows strict safety protocols and provides trained staff to supervise and guide the students throughout the trip.
2. Costs: The cost of the trip, including transportation, museum admission, and any related fees, will be covered by the school.
3. Behavior: Students are expected to maintain appropriate behavior and follow the instructions given by the teachers and museum staff. Failure to do so may result in the student being excluded from future field trips.
4. Chaperones: We require two parent chaperones to accompany the students on this trip. If you are interested in volunteering as a chaperone, please indicate below. Chaperones will be selected on a first-come, first-served basis and will need to undergo a brief screening process.

Please complete the permission slip below and return it to your child's teacher by [due date].

----------------------------------[Cut Here]------------------------------------

Figure 6.7   ChatGPT output with permission slip including places for parents to fill out key information.

to AI systems will reduce the amount of non-instructional work teachers must do without sacrificing our necessary policies and procedures.

[School Name]
[Address]
[City, State, ZIP]

I give permission for my child, [Student's Name], in [Grade/Class], to participate in the field trip to the Natural History Museum on March 1st.

Student Information:

* Student's Full Name: _____
* Grade/Class: _____

Emergency Contact Information:

* Parent/Guardian Name: _____
* Phone Number: _____
* Email: _____

Please indicate if you are interested in volunteering as a chaperone:
[ ] Yes, I am interested in being a chaperone.
[ ] No, I am unable to volunteer as a chaperone.

Parent/Guardian Signature: _____
Date: _____

-------------------------------------[Cut Here]-------------------------------------

Please ensure that this permission slip is completed and returned to your child's teacher by [due date]. If you have any questions or concerns, please feel free to contact me at [your contact information].

Thank you for your cooperation.

Sincerely,

[Your Name]
[Your Title/Role]
[Contact Information]

Figure 6.7 *(Continued)*

Prompt It!

OPTIMIZING PAPERWORK

- **Template:** "Generate a template for a weekly lesson plan that includes sections for objectives, materials, procedures, and assessment strategies."

- **Feedback Form:** "Create a standardized feedback form for student assignments that includes areas for strengths, areas for improvement, and specific action steps."

- **Grants:** "Draft an outline for a grant proposal for classroom resources focused on promoting STEM education."

- **Meeting Template:** "Create a template for meeting minutes for parent-teacher association meetings, including sections for attendees, key discussion points, decisions made, and action items."

RECORDKEEPING TASKS

- **Spreadsheet:** "Design a student progress tracking spreadsheet that includes sections for student names, assignments, scores, and areas for improvement."

- **Behavioral Incident Tracking:** "Generate a template for recording individual student behavior incidents, including sections for date, incident details, actions taken, and follow-up needed."

- **Attendance:** "Draft a template for a class attendance record that includes student names, dates, and attendance status (present, absent, tardy)."

- **System Design:** "Create a system for recording and tracking parent-teacher communication, including parent's name, student's name, date of communication, method (email, phone, etc.), and key points discussed."

- **Standardize Format:** "Provide a format for recording the minutes of faculty meetings, including attendees, agenda items, key discussions, decisions made, and next steps."

CONCLUSION

Reducing administrative tasks and burdens on teachers will be necessary as our country continues to face a teacher burnout crisis. The use of AI technology has the potential to dramatically reduce the time teachers spend on tasks that are cumbersome and time-consuming.

By helping educators communicate with all necessary stakeholders, it can ensure that everyone is appropriately involved. AI can help provide clear and consistent updates, support multilingual communication, and draft responses unaffected by personal emotion.

If AI is used for automated grading, it has the potential to offer unbiased and consistent feedback while freeing up teachers to dedicate more time to helping students act on the feedback. This opportunity to focus more on the human element of teaching will foster a more engaging learning environment for teachers and students.

Despite these advancements being the tip of the iceberg, they already indicate the monumental change AI could bring. As we continue to explore the implications of the age of AI on education, we should be open to these changes, adapt to them effectively, and leverage their potential benefits to create a more efficient educational system.

Exit Ticket

Take a recent email you sent that you dreaded writing a response to (or one still sitting in your inbox). Try to have an AI tool draft a response that is appropriate, accurate, and similar to something you might say in response. Maybe you can write one less email today!

Chapter 7

Boosting Engagement and Motivation

Student engagement and motivation are ongoing problems in education. Still, the advent of technology that captures students' attention, encourages short attention spans, and provides never-ending stimuli has worsened the situation. As a result, teachers are struggling to compete for students' attention. Although some will argue that that is not the responsibility of teachers, it is, unfortunately, at the least still our problem.

AI provides a golden opportunity to integrate technology into our classrooms in a way that directly contributes to learning and, in fact, is likely to make classroom instruction more effective. For example, the ability to personalize learning to be hyperspecific to our students' needs and interests will likely boost engagement and motivation. In addition, the ability to produce unique, innovative content in multiple formats will allow teachers to provide the type of engaging content our students seek.

Developments in AI bring with them the potential for intelligent tutoring systems that provide personalized, one-on-one support that provides targeted instruction and feedback. The ability for students to journey through personalized learning paths that align with their interests further helps increase student support. The ability to gamify the learning experience and make it active through debates and discussions helps redefine the learning experience as a rewarding and joyful experience. In addition, providing students with the support they need to improve their executive functioning and social-emotional awareness will likely pay dividends for years to come.

INTELLIGENT TUTORING SYSTEMS

- What are intelligent tutoring systems, and how do they work?
- How can intelligent tutoring systems enhance student engagement and motivation?
- How can educators effectively integrate intelligent tutoring systems into their teaching?

Intelligent tutoring systems (ITSs) are computer-based instructional systems that use AI to provide personalized learning experiences for students. They rely on multiple data sets and AI models to work with students the way a human tutor might. The four components of ITSs are:

- **Domain Model**: This is the information about the subject matter at hand. This includes facts, typical frameworks, assessments, learning objectives, and other information necessary for the ITS to have fluency in the topic being taught.

- **Student Model:** This is the key difference between an ITS and any other AI chatbot. The ITS forms a model of the student, constantly updating information about their knowledge, skills, and learning needs based on their interactions with the system.

- **Tutoring Model:** This part of the system focuses on pedagogy. It determines the most appropriate way to work with the student based on the student model and decides when to introduce new concepts, provide hints, correct mistakes, and offer feedback.

- **User Interface:** The end user sees this when interacting with the tutoring system. This includes the platform, any media or text it has, and generally, the entire interface through which the student accesses information and interacts with learning tools.

The key to an effective ITS is that, over time, it forms an understanding of the student's strengths, weaknesses, learning style, and pace. Using this information, it then caters the tutoring to match the student. For example, if a student struggles, the ITS might revisit foundational topics or present information using different phrasing or format.

Conversely, if a student is having an easy time with the material, it will provide more challenges so that the student doesn't become disengaged. The other benefit of using ITS is that they provide immediate feedback to the student. This enables them to quickly learn from mistakes and reinforce weak areas before progressing. Therefore, these systems can provide appropriate scaffolding to ensure the student has the support they need to build mastery while constantly pushing them to improve.

ITS can also preemptively adapt content and strategies based on what they have learned about a student. For example, if a student requires storytelling to understand a topic thoroughly, it will introduce new topics with storytelling. It can also customize the resources based on their needs and include accessibility features to support students with diverse learning needs. Advanced systems are also likely to adapt the assessments to ensure that the student is being tested on mastery of content rather than on how well the student can perform on a particular type of assessment.

ITS can be used across various subjects, making them versatile tools once they become popularized. While this technology may seem very off, most of it is already here. Some current tools that function as early-stage ITSs are:

- Khan Academy's Khanmigo provides students with one-on-one tutoring while they navigate through Khan Academy's video lessons.
- Duolingo teaches foreign languages using gamified lessons, adaptive feedback, and speech recognition to help students learn.
- Quizlet has a chatbot that aims to provide tutoring assistance, such as assessing writing skills and offering hints and explanations.
- Socrat.ai allows teachers to provide targeted tutoring assistance to students while monitoring their interactions.

In Figure 7.1, Socrat.ai engages with a student on the main idea and provides instant feedback and more examples to help the student identify a main idea.

Students can also engage with generative AI bots to offer some of the same support and tutoring that more robust ITS can. For example, they can ask ChatGPT for help understanding how to do long division or provide Bard with a draft of their essay and ask for feedback.

As the technology matures, the tutoring systems will be closer to full-fledged ITS that can hold context between interactions and tutors on various topics.

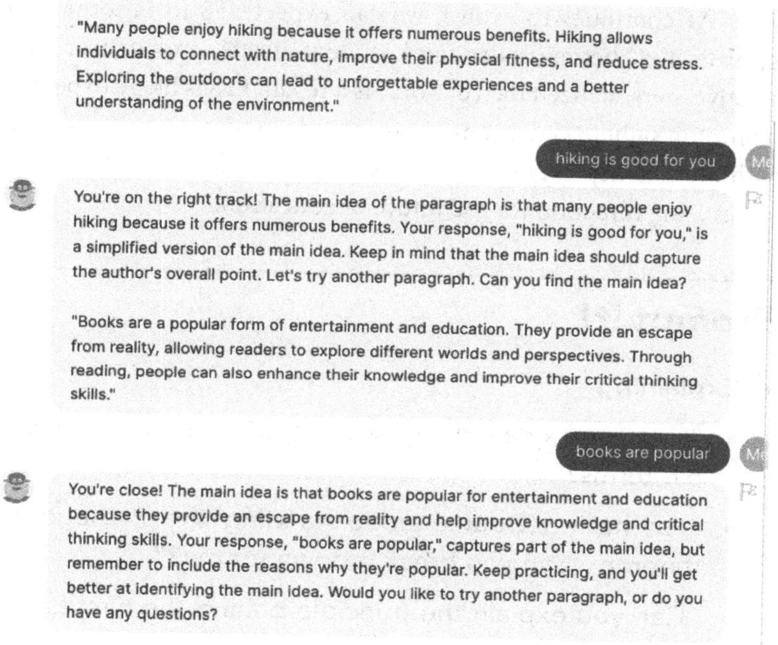

"Many people enjoy hiking because it offers numerous benefits. Hiking allows individuals to connect with nature, improve their physical fitness, and reduce stress. Exploring the outdoors can lead to unforgettable experiences and a better understanding of the environment."

hiking is good for you

You're on the right track! The main idea of the paragraph is that many people enjoy hiking because it offers numerous benefits. Your response, "hiking is good for you," is a simplified version of the main idea. Keep in mind that the main idea should capture the author's overall point. Let's try another paragraph. Can you find the main idea?

"Books are a popular form of entertainment and education. They provide an escape from reality, allowing readers to explore different worlds and perspectives. Through reading, people can also enhance their knowledge and improve their critical thinking skills."

books are popular

You're close! The main idea is that books are popular for entertainment and education because they provide an escape from reality and help improve knowledge and critical thinking skills. Your response, "books are popular," captures part of the main idea, but remember to include the reasons why they're popular. Keep practicing, and you'll get better at identifying the main idea. Would you like to try another paragraph, or do you have any questions?

Figure 7.1   Socrat.ai screenshot of a study session with a student on the topic of main idea.

Furthermore, while AI is advancing rapidly, creating a truly "intelligent" tutor that can replicate all the nuances of human teaching is still a work in progress. And while ITS can handle many instructional tasks, educators must remain part of the process for student support. Educators must also carefully evaluate and choose ITS that aligns with their curriculum and instructional goals. Once ITS is implemented, educators should regularly review student data generated by the ITS to inform instructional decisions and provide additional support as needed. They should also combine ITS with traditional teaching methods to offer a blended approach and provide guidance and support to students.

As AI continues to evolve, we can expect ITS to become more sophisticated, better understand student needs, and deliver more effective, personalized instruction. As a result, ITS is likely to become a common sight in classrooms, homes, and anywhere learning occurs. With their ability to tailor instruction to individual needs, ITS offers a promising direction for the future of education.

Prompt It!

- **Explaining**
  - "Can you explain the concept of photosynthesis in simple terms?"
  - "I'm having trouble understanding the Pythagorean theorem. Can you break it down for me?"
  - "Can you explain the principle behind the First Law of Thermodynamics?"

- **Scaffolding**
  - "Can you give me feedback on this paragraph for my English assignment?"
  - "Can you guide me through the steps to solve a quadratic equation?"
  - "Can you provide a step-by-step guide for writing a persuasive essay?"
  - "I'm unsure how to start a research project on the American Civil War. Can you help me outline the steps?"

- **Suggesting**
  - "I need a topic for my history project. Can you suggest some interesting ones?"

- "I'm struggling to remember the elements of the periodic table. Do you have any memorization tips?"

- "Can you suggest some resources to learn more about coding in Python?"

- **Connecting**

  - "Can you provide an example of a metaphor in English literature?"

  - "I need help understanding the concept of supply and demand in economics. Can you use an analogy to explain?"

  - "Can you give me an example of how the law of conservation of energy works in a real-life situation?"

- **Quizzing**

  - "Can you quiz me on the capitals of the world?"

  - "I have a biology test coming up on human anatomy. Can you help me review some questions?"

  - "Can you help me create a flashcard set for French vocabulary words?"

PERSONALIZED LEARNING PATHWAYS

- What are the benefits of personalized learning pathways for students?

- What challenges do educators face when implementing personalized learning pathways?

- How can AI support personalized learning pathways?

Personalized learning pathways are another conceptual model of instruction that is becoming increasingly possible to implement in classrooms. Personal learning pathways tailor instruction to students' interests, preferences, and abilities. This differs from ITS because while ITS customizes "how" students learn, personalized learning pathways are designed to customize "what" students learn.

Moving away from standardized curriculum and material would allow us to boost student engagement while ensuring they are still learning important skills and dispositions that will serve them well in the age of AI. Students will be able to learn material aligned with their interests and goals and stay motivated and engaged as they explore opportunities to build on their knowledge.

The pace of learning can also be customized to the student's needs so that students who want to learn faster can do so if they are mastering content. Students who need to slow down to address learning gaps can also take the time to focus on long-term retention of information rather than arbitrary external deadlines.

In order to implement personalized learning paths within the traditional education system, educators can find ways to use some of the same principles and practices in their classrooms. First, educators should determine the core learning objectives and standards that are non-negotiable from the current curriculum. They should then allow students to define their learning goals and interests within those objectives. Teachers can then combine personalized learning pathways with traditional teaching methods while ensuring that the curriculum requirements are met. Students can then take mini detours to learn things that interest them while they still meet the necessary standards.

While most educators support some integration of personalized learning pathways, the constraints of traditional classrooms make it difficult to implement them. For example, teachers need more time to design and support students in crafting pathways. They also have limited tools, materials, and external support to ensure robust educational pathways. In addition, the number of students in a typical classroom can make it daunting.

Introducing AI systems (similar in concept to ITS) can help teachers effectively overcome those obstacles. AI systems can support students by suggesting different options for learning pathways, suggesting activities and resources that support learning, providing feedback and guidance as they work through the pathways, and assessing the students' mastery before moving on to the next topic.

In order to implement personalized learning pathways with AI, educators should choose AI tools that let them exercise some degree of control to ensure that curricular goals are still met. They should also choose platforms that provide data on student learning and progress and allow educators to intervene and tailor the pathway based on their own experience and expertise.

Prompt It!

- **Choosing**

  - "Can you suggest some questions I can ask myself to discover my learning interests and strengths?"

  - "I'm interested in wildlife. What careers could I consider?"

  - "I enjoy coding. What subjects should I focus on to become a software developer?"

- **Planning**

  - "What are the key topics I should cover to learn about astrophysics at a college level?"

  - "What online courses would you recommend for learning data science?"

- "How should I structure my study plan to learn French in the next six months?"
- "Can you suggest a step-by-step plan to learn digital painting?"

- **Crafting**
  - "What interesting programming projects can I work on to improve my coding skills?"
  - "What practical experiments can I try at home to understand physics better?"
  - "Can you help me develop a daily study routine to learn machine learning?"

- **Implementing**
  - "Can you help me understand the concept of photosynthesis in biology?"
  - "Can you provide some practice problems related to algebra?"
  - "Can you give me a summary of *To Kill a Mockingbird*?"

- **Assessing**
  - "Can you help me review the key concepts in American history?"
  - "Can you provide a self-assessment quiz for organic chemistry?"
  - "Based on my questions about quantum physics, what areas do you think I should focus on more?"

GAMIFICATION AND LEARNING EXPERIENCES

- What are the benefits of gamification for student engagement and motivation?
- How can AI enhance gamification strategies in the classroom?
- What are some examples of AI-powered educational games?

Gamification can make learning more enjoyable and engaging, and increase student motivation and participation. Even the students who think they are "too cool" for gamified learning end up enjoying and participating in gamified learning experiences. Typical features of gamification, like rewards, challenges, and progress tracking, push students to work harder and learn the material to excel at the games. In addition, gamification can often promote teamwork and collaboration as students work together to achieve shared goals or compete in friendly challenges.

AI can help with gamification both in the classroom and through custom platforms.

Through digital tools, AI can be integrated into gamified experiences that adjust game difficulty and content in real time to keep challenging students. AI tools can also generate new game content, challenges, or scenarios tailored to learning goals and student performance.

Educators can ensure they are making the most of AI-powered educational games by seeking games that complement existing curricula and can be easily integrated into lesson plans. They should also choose games where they can track student progress and learning and monitor students' retention of key curricular material. They should also provide opportunities for students to reflect on their learning and connect with their personal and classroom learning objectives.

Some ways AI can be used to gamify learning include:

- **Language learning games:** AI-powered language learning games, such as Duolingo, provide adaptive content and personalized feedback to help learners develop language skills.

- **Math and science games:** AI-powered games, like Prodigy, can adapt to individual student skill levels and provide targeted practice and feedback.

- **Coding games:** Educational games that teach programming skills, such as CodeCombat, can use AI to provide unique gamified experiences.

- **Brain training games:** AI-driven cognitive training games can offer personalized exercises to improve memory, attention, and problem-solving skills.

- **Virtual simulations:** AI-powered virtual simulations can provide dynamic learning experiences that adapt to individual student choices and actions.

Virtual simulations that combine artificial or virtual reality with AI can bring a deeper level of engagement by creating immersive, multi-dimensional environments. They can provide life-like simulations and interactive experiences, making learning more captivating. Students could, for example, take a virtual tour of a historical site, perform complex science experiments in a simulated lab, or explore the cosmos from their classroom. These would match the level of stimulation students receive from other domains and provide them with real-world experiences without leaving the classroom.

Finally, AI can also gamify the classroom by generating fun activities that complement curricular goals. For example, AI can make matching games and role-playing scenarios, generate narratives, and design classroom quizzing games.

Gamification will increasingly be necessary, and AI can support educators in helping make learning fun and engaging for their students.

Prompt It!

- **Short Story:** "Generate a short story in which the characters have to use algebra to solve a problem."

- **Context Shifting:** "Describe a historical event as if it were a level in a video game."

- **Quest:** "Design a quest where a group of explorers has to use the scientific method to solve a problem."

- **Classroom Game:** "Create a game where players level up by correctly answering biology questions."

- **Role-Play:** "Create a dialogue for a role-playing game where characters debate a moral issue from a literature book."

- **Treasure Hunt:** "Invent a geography-based treasure hunt game."

- **Simulation:** "Describe a classroom simulation game that helps players understand the stock market."

- **Choose-Your-Own-Adventure:** "Create a choose-your-own-adventure story that explores different cultures worldwide."

- **Mission Games:** "Write a mission briefing for a spy game where the agent has to understand the constitutions of different countries."

- **Escape Room:** "Plan a classroom escape room that incorporates concepts from geometry."

DEBATES AND DISCUSSIONS

- How can AI help educators design engaging debate topics and prompts?
- How can AI assist in structuring classroom debates and discussions for maximum engagement?
- How can educators use AI to ensure diverse perspectives and ideas are included in debates and discussions?

Students will continue to need the persuasion and communication skills that debate teaches. As classrooms become sites of more active learning, debates and discussions are an easy way to incorporate more student voices and AI-proof assignments into the classroom.

AI tools can help teachers design engaging topics and prompts depending on the classroom goals and objectives. For example, AI tools can suggest topics based on current events, match the complexity of issues to the subject and grade level, incorporate diverse perspectives, and align with the curriculum.

AI tools can also help teachers plan student groupings for discussions, scaffold discussions with preparation guides and prompts, and provide rubrics to assess student performance. As AI tools are further integrated, they can help moderate debates, track participation, and even intervene to guide the discussion or ask provoking questions. They will then generate feedback, identify strengths and weaknesses based on the interaction, and provide it to students.

Including AI tools in setting up and monitoring debates and discussions can also help avoid potential bias. AI tools can search and curate diverse resources, including articles, videos, and podcasts, representing multiple viewpoints for students to explore. AI tools can also generate sample arguments and counterarguments from various views to provide diverse perspectives. Future AI tools can also serve as moderators and ensure that inappropriate or factual inaccuracies are addressed immediately.

Students can also debate AI bots, practicing their argumentation skills with the AI bot as their opponent. In doing so, students can receive immediate feedback and hone their skills without fear of judgment. In addition, the AI bot could argue from different perspectives, allowing students to engage with various viewpoints.

Student Debates Bot

Prompt: "I want to debate with you about whether wind or solar energy is better. Choose a stance and present your argument."

Bard presents a complete argument and some rhetorical additions at the end (see Figure 7.2). The student can then go back and forth with responses to engage in the debate.

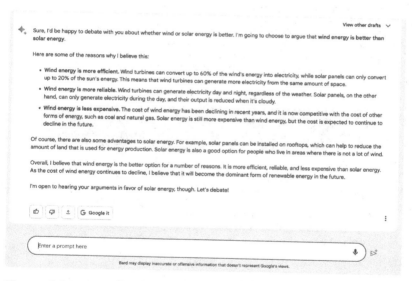

Figure 7.2   Google Bard output with an argument in favor of wind energy.

Special tools tailor-made for debating with AI also exist. For example, Socrat.ai allows teachers to assign a custom topic for students to debate with Socrat.ai on.

In Figure 7.3, Socrat.ai models respectfully disagreeing with your opponent and provides direct responses to the student's arguments.

Given all these possibilities, AI can be instrumental in crafting and facilitating engaging debate topics, structuring classroom discussions, and ensuring diverse perspectives are represented in these intellectual exchanges.

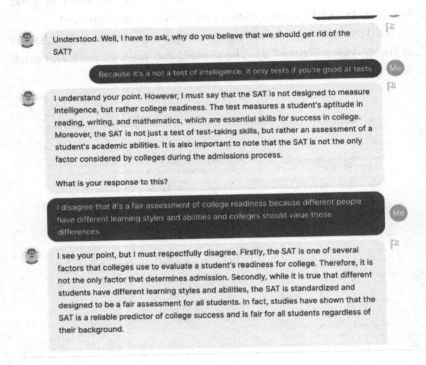

Figure 7.3 Socrat.ai screenshot of a debate with a student on the topic of the SAT.

Prompt It!

- Topics

  - "Generate five debate topics related to climate change. Make sure these topics consider diverse perspectives and are suitable for grade 10 students."

  - "Generate a list of current event-based discussion topics appropriate for grade 8 students studying social sciences."

  - "Provide a debate topic that explores the ethical considerations surrounding the use of genetic engineering in modern medicine. Also, generate three main points for and against this topic."

- Structure

  - "Construct a structured format for a classroom debate, including timing, speaker roles, and transitions for grade 11 students debating the pros and cons of social media."

  - "Provide a step-by-step discussion guide to facilitate a group discussion on the topic of 'Racial Inequality in America' for a high school sociology class."

- Diverse Perspectives

  - "Generate an array of potential perspectives on the topic of 'Universal Basic Income' for our upcoming class discussion."

  - "Provide a balanced overview of the viewpoints related to 'Animal Testing in the Cosmetics Industry', ensuring to include perspectives from animal rights activists, industry professionals, and consumers."

- **Debating with AI**
  - "Act as a debater supporting the motion 'Online Learning Is More Effective than Traditional Classroom Learning.' Provide key points and examples to strengthen your argument and respond to my arguments afterward."
  - "In a debate about 'Genetically Modified Foods,' play the role of a debater arguing in favor of this technology. Offer points related to factors like food security, climate change, and agricultural productivity, and respond to my counterarguments."
  - "Debate with me on {fill}."

EXECUTIVE FUNCTIONING AND SOCIAL-EMOTIONAL LEARNING

- How can AI support the development of self-regulation and metacognition?
- How can AI support the development of executive functioning?
- How can AI help assess and track social-emotional learning skills?

Students who struggle in school and beyond often have underdeveloped executive function or social-emotional skills (SEL). Schools are increasingly focusing on helping students gain these skills, but the level of individual focus they require has proven to be a hurdle.

AI can help students gain these skills by acting as a personal companion as they go through their daily routines. AI bots will have the advantage of being able to cater skill development to the unique needs of each student by providing appropriate resources and guidance based on conversations and data. They will also be able to intervene quickly and provide real-time feedback to help reorient students.

AI tools can also help teachers create resources to support their students as they gain these skills. For example, it can help teachers develop reflective questions and activities to encourage students to think about their executive functioning and SEL skills in various contexts.

AI bots can help students set realistic, achievable self-regulation and metacognitive development goals so that they are in charge of their own skill development. AI tools will then be able to track student progress in self-regulation and metacognition and provide regular updates and feedback on performance. Based on the data, AI can then suggest personalized strategies and interventions to the students and even help provide them with tools to self-assess, helping students develop self-awareness and personal responsibility.

AI bots can also continuously assess student performance in executive functioning and SEL tasks using sentiment analysis and conversation data. AI bots can detect potential challenges or skill gaps in executive functioning and SEL and provide timely support and intervention or guide educators.

AI-based simulations and scenario-based learning can help students learn and practice these skills. For example, AI can generate role-playing scenarios where students must use their executive functioning and social-emotional skills to practice in a controlled environment. AI technology will also support peer-to-peer interaction. For example, platforms that promote group discussions can monitor student interactions and highlight areas where social-emotional learning can improve.

Overall, AI has the potential to help students develop essential skills for life through personalized, adaptive, and comprehensive support that will empower students to take control of their own growth and development.

Prompt It!

SELF-REGULATION AND METACOGNITION

- **Teacher Prompts**

    - **Journal:** "Generate a daily reflective journal template that students can use to track their learning process and understand their thinking patterns."

    - **Self-Evaluation:** "Design a series of questions that students can ask themselves to evaluate their understanding of a new concept."

    - **Guide:** "Create a guide that explains various self-regulation strategies for studying, including how and when to use them."

- **Student Prompts**

    - **Blind Spots:** "Based on my current understanding of the Pythagorean theorem, what are some potential areas I might be misunderstanding?"

    - **Scaffold:** "Describe how I would solve a complex math problem. What steps should I take, and what questions should I ask myself along the way?"

    - **Strategies:** "What strategies can I use to regulate my emotions while studying for a challenging exam?"

EXECUTIVE FUNCTIONING

- **Teacher Prompts**

    - **Project Planning:** "Create a project management template that students can use to break down assignments into manageable tasks."

- **Lesson:** "Outline a lesson on time management strategies, including examples and practice exercises."
- **Student Prompts**
  - **Strategy:** "What practical strategy can I use to improve my focus during study sessions?"
  - **Schedule:** "Help me create a study schedule for the upcoming week, considering my other commitments."
  - **Chunk:** "How can I effectively break down a large research project into smaller, manageable tasks?"

SOCIAL-EMOTIONAL LEARNING SKILLS
- **Teacher Prompts**
  - **Role-Play:** "Compose a series of role-play scenarios to help students practice empathy and understanding in diverse situations."
  - **Case Study:** "Design a lesson plan on conflict resolution, including case studies and practical exercises."
  - **Guided Meditation:** "Create a guided meditation script focused on managing stress and building resilience."
- **Student Prompts**
  - **Perspective-Taking:** "Describe techniques I can use to understand the perspectives of others better."
  - **Tips:** "Provide advice on how to manage my stress during exam season."
  - **Strategy:** "What steps can I take to communicate my feelings in conflicts effectively?"

CONCLUSION

Our classrooms' complex student engagement and motivation issues, exacerbated by increased attention-demanding technology, necessitate innovative solutions.

AI presents itself as a promising tool to transform these dynamics. It offers the capacity to personalize learning experiences, thus making them intrinsically captivating and attuned to individual student needs and interests.

In addition, it increases the potential for intelligent tutoring systems that offer personalized, immediate feedback, aligning learning paths with students' intrinsic motivations.

The capacity to gamify learning and foster interactive experiences adapts our classrooms into places of joy and curiosity. Additionally, AI's support in promoting students' executive functioning and social-emotional awareness will have long-term benefits.

It is, thus, crucial to leverage AI's capabilities in education to bridge the gap between the digital world's distractions and the genuine, meaningful learning that our students are capable of.

Exit Ticket

Think about one of the ways outlined in this chapter to create an engaging classroom environment for students. Choose some of the prompts and combine them with your own curricular goals and classroom practices to generate a plan to increase student engagement in your classroom. Try to focus on one unit at a time.

Chapter 8

Teaching Students about AI

Our students not only need to know how to learn with AI, but also they need to learn about AI. As AI becomes more prevalent in every aspect of their lives, they need the skills and knowledge to safely and effectively navigate the changes in our society. Students with AI literacy skills will be able to make informed decisions about using AI-powered tools and services and be empowered to actively participate in shaping the future of technology to align with societal values and needs.

In addition, exposure to the responsible use of AI can help dispel misconceptions, fears, and hype surrounding the technology. Despite debates on its potential misuse, providing students with practical experience using and interacting with AI can help build habits that will serve them long term. The reality is that our world will be powered by AI technology, and if we are to prepare students to enter the world, they must develop fluency with the tools and services available to them.

Conversations about ethics and AI should be integrated throughout our curricula to reinforce the norms and values that will create responsible students. We should also instill civic values in our students that help them navigate the changing world of digital citizenship and misinformation. Students should also be empowered to refine and iterate on AI-generated content, be influential users of AI technology, and contribute meaningfully to society. The saying, "AI won't replace us, but someone who knows how to use AI will," holds. We must ensure our students have the necessary knowledge and skills to avoid displacement.

RESPONSIBLE AND ETHICAL USE OF AI

- What are the principles of responsible AI use in education?
- How can educators model ethical AI use for their students?
- How can schools develop policies and guidelines for responsible AI use?

Concerns over the unethical use of AI have caused backlash from educators concerned about students misusing AI to cheat on school assignments. The responsibility lies with us to ensure that students are educated on the ethical and responsible use of AI so that they can see AI as a tool to help them learn and grow rather than avoid hard work. Some fundamental principles of responsible use that educators should emphasize include:

- **Honesty:** Students should use AI tools to aid their thinking and learning, not as a replacement for hard work.
- **Privacy:** Students should consider the importance of their privacy and how AI impacts it.
- **Equity:** Students should be aware of the potential biases in AI systems.

- **Humanity:** Students should understand the limits of AI technology, and they should be able to identify where human intervention is necessary.

- **Adaptation:** Students should commit to lifelong learning about AI and its implications on their lives and the rest of society.

Educators will also need to model responsible and ethical use of AI to their students in how they approach using it themselves. Schools should strive for:

- **Transparency:** Be open and honest about the use of AI in the classroom.

- **Fairness:** Strive to use AI applications in a way that is fair for all students.

- **Privacy and data protection:** Make sure to safeguard sensitive student information.

- **Inclusivity:** Accommodate diverse learning needs and preferences in choosing AI tools.

- **Humanity:** Use AI to augment human interactions rather than replace them.

Educators will need to build robust policies at the school and classroom levels to ensure that responsible and ethical use of AI is encouraged and required. In forming these policies, educators should work with other relevant stakeholders, including students and parents, to ensure that the guidelines reflect diverse perspectives and needs. They should also comply with district policy and legal regulations concerning data privacy and accessibility. Teachers will also need to advocate for support from their schools, including professional development, implementation support from technology specialists, and supporting policies and guidelines publicly.

In developing these policies, teachers should reflect on the following questions and ensure that students and parents understand the reasoning behind the policies:

- What is the primary purpose of using AI in the classroom?
  - Is it to assist teachers or enhance learning for students?
  - How will it improve teaching and learning processes?
- How will privacy and data security be safeguarded?
  - What data will the AI system collect from students?
  - Who will access the collected data, and how will it be used?
- What are the potential risks of using AI in the classroom?
  - How will we address biases?
  - Will diverse students have equal access and benefits?
- How will we ensure that AI is used ethically?
  - How will we prevent the misuse of AI tools for cheating, plagiarism, or other unethical activities?
  - How will we ensure that AI does not hinder critical thinking and problem-solving skills?
- How will we involve all stakeholders?
  - How will we communicate the use of AI to students, parents, and other staff members?
  - How will we obtain informed consent where necessary?

Classroom Policy

You can even draft a policy by providing these questions and quick answers to ChatGPT!

Prompt: "Draft a classroom AI policy addressing the following questions and my notes."

Classroom AI Policy

1. The main purpose of using AI in the classroom is to enhance learning for students and assist teachers. AI technologies have the potential to revolutionize education by providing personalized learning experiences, offering intelligent tutoring, and automating administrative tasks, among other benefits. The integration of AI in the classroom aims to improve student engagement, academic performance, and overall educational outcomes.

2. Privacy and data security will be of utmost importance and safeguarded through the following measures:

   a. The AI system will collect only relevant and necessary data from students to support their learning and provide personalized experiences. This may include information such as academic performance, progress, and learning preferences.

   b. Collected data will be securely stored and transmitted using industry-standard encryption and other appropriate security measures.

   c. Access to student data will be strictly limited to authorized personnel, such as teachers and administrators, who require the information to perform their educational duties.

   d. The collected data will be used solely for educational purposes, such as adapting instructional content, monitoring progress, and improving the effectiveness of the AI system. It will not be shared with third parties for commercial purposes without explicit consent.

3. Potential risks of using AI in the classroom will be addressed proactively, considering the following aspects:

   a. Biases in AI algorithms will be mitigated through rigorous testing, validation, and continuous monitoring. Efforts will be made to ensure that AI systems are designed and trained to be fair, unbiased, and inclusive.

   b. Diverse students will have equal access to AI technologies and benefits, regardless of their background, abilities, or characteristics. Special considerations will be given to address any potential biases or disparities.

Figure 8.1 ChatGPT output of an AI policy for the classroom based on the preceding questions.

In Figure 8.1, you can see that ChatGPT is rather ambitious about the safeguards that will be put in place for responsible AI usage, but it offers a starting point for you to build your classroom policy.

Relying on external tools and platforms to monitor AI-based cheating is futile. These platforms and tools can easily be outsmarted, often using the same algorithms that the creators use to detect the AI-generated text, and no tool has anywhere near the level of certainty that would be appropriate for a tool that will be used to decide

4. The ethical use of AI in the classroom will be prioritized with the following measures:

a. Adequate safeguards will be implemented to prevent misuse of AI tools for cheating, plagiarism, or any other unethical activities. Monitoring systems may be put in place to detect and deter such behavior.

b. AI technologies will be designed to complement and enhance critical thinking and problem-solving skills, rather than replacing them. Emphasis will be placed on fostering creativity, independent thought, and collaboration among students.

5. All stakeholders, including students, parents, and staff members, will be involved and informed about the use of AI in the following ways:

a. Transparent communication channels will be established to keep all stakeholders informed about the purpose, benefits, and potential impact of AI in the classroom.

b. Students and parents will be provided with clear explanations of how AI technologies will be utilized, what data will be collected, and how it will be used. Informed consent will be obtained when necessary, and individuals will have the right to opt-out or request the deletion of their data.

c. Professional development programs will be conducted for teachers and staff members to ensure they are equipped with the necessary knowledge and skills to effectively use AI tools in their instructional practices.

d. Ongoing feedback mechanisms will be established to gather input, concerns, and suggestions from stakeholders, fostering a collaborative approach to the use of AI in education.

Figure 8.1 *(Continued)*

consequences for students. We must instead focus on helping students engage with their learning process authentically rather than use unreliable tools to play police with how they use AI.

Thus, you must also amend or add an academic integrity policy to ensure that AI usage is productive, not detrimental to learning. Here are some questions you should ask when crafting these policies:

- **Tools:** Are there specific tools students are not allowed to use or should exclusively use?
- **Role:** What parts of the work can AI be used for? Can they use it to brainstorm, research, outline, draft content, edit their work, and so on?
- **Support:** Will you provide students without prior exposure to AI support or resources to help them use allowed tools?

- **Work product:** What will be considered the final work product assessed? Will students be evaluated on work products that could be AI-generated without detection, or will assessment shift to in-classroom projects like oral presentations and Socratic seminars?

Different institutions have taken different approaches, including banning AI altogether, encouraging usage for brainstorming, and citing AI as a source. Whatever policy you choose, you should make sure it is fair, transparent, and enforceable. Overly authoritative guidelines are unlikely to be enforceable and more likely to assess students based on AI literacy rather than content knowledge. The longer-term sustainable strategy will have to encourage self-motivated learning and demonstrate content expertise and skills in controlled environments.

DIGITAL CITIZENSHIP IN THE AI ERA

- How has the concept of digital citizenship evolved with the rise of AI?

- What digital citizenship skills are essential for students in the AI era?

- How can educators address online safety and privacy issues related to AI?

Students will need to use AI responsibly within and outside the classroom. Digital citizenship will continue to increase in scope as more civic discourse and action take place on the internet. The advent of social media dramatically changed how and where public discourse occurs, and AI will likely complicate discussions in the public sphere further.

Developing AI literacy will be essential for digital citizens to navigate an increasingly AI-driven world effectively. They will need the ability to advocate for fair and responsible rules and regulations with their representatives, fight against platforms that use AI unethically to spread misinformation, and identify biases in algorithms that perpetuate echo chambers. In addition, our students will need to actively participate in shaping technology's development to ensure it aligns with societal values. To do that, they must have engaged in robust education about civic values, ethos and AI technology.

Students will need to thoroughly understand the potential for bias in AI systems and the ability to spot them through refined critical thinking skills, including the ability to spot logical fallacies and cognitive biases.

In an increasingly digital world, we will need to teach students how to practice respectful and empathetic communication in online, AI-enhanced environments and consider the feelings and perspectives of others. They will need active listening skills and open-mindedness to ensure they can value diverse views and opinions and not allow AI-powered content to feed into their preconceived notions about society.

Schools can help develop digital citizens by establishing and communicating clear online safety and privacy guidelines. In addition, fundamental digital citizenship skills like creating secure passwords, recognizing phishing attempts, and managing personal information online will continue to grow in importance. Identifying and spotting cyberbullying and other forms of malicious digital behavior will also be central to digital citizenship.

Schools can lead the charge for better digital citizenship by:

- **Involving parents:** Students engage with technology inside and outside the classroom, and ensuring that parents are on the same page about supporting their children's digital citizenship will provide consistent messaging.

- **Integrating:** Integrating digital citizenship concepts and skills whenever digital tools are used can help build the dispositions through practice and reinforcements.

- **Modeling:** Teachers can model responsible digital citizenship and explicitly call attention to behaviors and patterns they expect students to learn.

Teachers should make sure to encourage critical thinking and openly discuss the limitations and biases of technology through open dialogue with students. This can happen through many different mediums:

- **Ethics education:** Focus on AI and its impact on society during conversations about ethics.

- **Real-world example:** Provide AI stories about both the positive and negative implications of AI.

- **Debates and discussions:** Foster open dialogue with students about the responsible use of AI.

- **Reflection:** Have students reflect on their own experiences and interactions with AI.

Teachers can engage on these topics from multiple different angles and subtopics. Here are some interesting implications of AI to explore:

- **Bias:** What are some ways we can fight bias in AI?

- **Job displacement:** Should governments regulate AI to prevent mass job displacement due to automation?

- **Policing:** Is the use of AI in predictive policing ethical?

- **Weapons:** Should AI be used in autonomous weapons systems?

- **Healthcare:** Is using AI to diagnose diseases and predict health risks ethical?

- **Decision-making:** Should AI systems be designed to explain their decisions and actions?

- **Advertising:** Is using AI to create personalized ads an invasion of privacy or a convenient feature?

- **Education:** Should AI systems replace human teachers for customized learning?
- **Deep fakes:** Is the creation and use of deep fakes ever ethically acceptable?
- **Regulations:** Should international laws and regulations control the development and use of AI?
- **Face recognition:** Is using AI-powered facial recognition systems by governments and private entities ethical?
- **Justice:** Should AI be used in predicting criminal behavior and assisting in judgments?
- **Self-driving cars:** How should AI be programmed to behave in self-driving cars?
- **Privacy:** What level of privacy should we expect in a society powered by AI?

For case studies, lesson plans, and worksheets on these topics, you can visit pedagog.ai.

REFINING AND ITERATING ON AI-GENERATED CONTENT

- How can students be encouraged to engage critically with AI-generated content?
- What skills and strategies are necessary for evaluating and improving AI-generated content?
- How can educators teach students to refine and iterate on AI-generated content?

Teachers are already starting to help students learn AI literacy and develop the skills to productively engage with AI output by having students produce AI output and then refine or iterate on it.

This way of integrating AI into the classroom is a great starting point for conversations on all the limitations of AI, including biases, factual inaccuracies because of hallucinations, and misunderstanding of the nuances of human thinking.

Teachers should help students learn how to approach reading AI-generated output by:

- **Questioning:** Students should be encouraged to approach AI output with a questioning mindset. How can they verify the truth of the output rather than assume it is true just by looking at it?

- **Improvement:** Students should be able to think actively about what areas of the output they would improve. How can they make what the AI created better?

- **Collaborate:** Students should be encouraged to think about ways to use AI output to streamline work with their peers. For example, how can they take AI outputs and productively devise a solution together?

- **Reflect:** Students should reflect on how their questions and prompts influenced the AI's output. For example, what could they have said more clearly to produce better output from the AI tool?

- **Feedback:** Students should know to follow up with AI tools and ask for revisions based on their judgments about the flaws in the content.

- **Compare:** Students can compare output generated by AI to output they would generate, or other humans have generated, to begin to spot the strengths and weaknesses of AI.

Here are a few sample assignments that teachers can use to incorporate AI iterating in their classrooms:

- **ELA:** Students can have AI draft a story, and then they have to tweak it based on a random phrase they pick out of a hat.

For example, the phrases might include "Change the setting to 100 years earlier" or "Incorporate guacamole as a key component of the climax."

- **History:** Students can ask AI to generate a historical narrative, and then they can check it for accuracy or back it up with primary sources.

- **Math:** Students and AI can both solve a word problem and show their work step by step, and students can compare how the steps differ.

- **Science:** Students can ask AI to develop a hypothesis that a student could easily test, and then the student can design an experiment to test the theory.

- **Art:** Students can have AI create art mimicking a particular painter, and then the students can critique what the artist might have done differently.

- **Journalism:** Students can have the AI generate an op-ed on a current event, and then they can write a letter to the editor in response.

One of the significant concerns that teachers have is about writing essays. While essay writing is likely to be devalued as generative AI tools become the norm for producing polished writing, the essential skills of researching and thinking about relevant topics will still be an important part of the learning journey for students. To help students responsibly integrate AI into the writing process, teachers can offer some or all of the following suggestions:

- **Brainstorming:** Students can use AI tools to brainstorm topics, potential arguments on both sides, and particular analogies or examples that might be useful.

- **Researching:** Students can start their research with AI tools that can search the internet and share other relevant resources.

- **Summarizing:** Students can use AI tools to distill the main points from a lengthy source.

- **Outlining:** Students can have AI generate an initial outline for their writing.

- **Drafting:** Students can have AI generate a first draft of their writing.

- **Editing:** Students can provide their writing to AI tools to get feedback and suggestions.

Teachers will want to choose one or some of these stages to encourage students to use AI tools or even allow them to choose which stage they incorporate AI into. Asking students to submit work as they go along, to write in a word processor that tracks changes (like Google Docs), and to provide the prompts and changes they made can all help teachers hold students accountable for participating in the iterative process of writing. Even a student who uses AI for all of these stages will learn about the topic and think critically to prompt the AI tool and refine and iterate on what the AI bot is generating.

Students need to learn how to effectively work with AI rather than have AI do their work for them. However, the skill set of using AI to augment their work process will be instrumental when they enter the workforce and can work efficiently while still providing value to the institutions they become members of.

ADDRESSING AI-RELATED MISINFORMATION AND BIAS

- How can educators foster open discussions about AI-related misinformation and bias?

- How can educators teach students to be responsible consumers and producers of AI-generated content?

- What are the implications of AI-related misinformation and bias for digital citizenship?

AI-related misinformation and bias are significant concerns for the ethical use of AI in our society. As AI systems become better at mimicking humans in every way, the potential for a bad actor to take advantage of the technology to spread misinformation and manipulate people is a real threat to social stability.

Educators will need to establish spaces where students can comfortably engage in dialogue about what is considered misinformation, what biases are problematic, and what implications that has for how AI is used. In addition, they should provide real-world examples to help students understand the threat and learn to be wary of anything that multiple sources cannot verify.

Some of the previous sections offer steps to help students learn how to engage with AI content both as consumers and producers ethically. For example, the media literacy skills students have been learning about fake news and misinformation will need to be strengthened to withstand a new generation of misinformation. In addition, they will have to be ethical producers of output that is not used to manipulate or mislead others and develop the proper dispositions and civic ethos by understanding the consequences.

Parents will also have to be engaged in the discussions around misinformation to ensure that parents can discuss these issues at home and help students spot instances of it. They must also help students learn the consequences of spreading misinformation, especially cyberbullying.

Students will have the responsibility to help create healthy and trustworthy digital environments, and working with them to craft what that means and how to safeguard them will be critical components of education in the age of AI. In addition, students will need the skills to monitor their online safety, practice empathy and inclusivity in how they approach others, and stay informed about technology's growing capabilities.

AI technology can already create all kinds of misinformation through different mediums.

Words

AI-generated text can be made to sound like a particular person. For example, ChatGPT produces the following fake speech when prompted.

Prompt: "Draft a 100-word speech on AI and misinformation as if Donald Trump wrote it."

> Ladies and Gentlemen, AI is incredible, it really is. But there's a problem — it's also spreading fake news. Tremendous amounts of misinformation. It's not good folks, not good. We must ensure AI tells us the truth. It needs to be better, smarter. Like us. We deserve that. Let's demand AI we can trust, AI that makes America great again. Thank you.

Creating believable letters, quotes, and other text that mimics a particular person increases the likelihood that someone will believe the misinformation.

With technology that can make voices sound like real people and videos that look real even with lip movement, the potential to make it appear as if someone has said something is incredibly high.

Photo

AI can even create photo-realistic images that can deceive people into believing that a particular event or situation actually occurred.

Prompt: "/imagine a hyper-realistic photograph of Mark Zuckerburg and Barack Obama dancing in front of the White House, Leica 50mm, Kodak portra 800, chiaroscuro, f1. 4, --ar 4:3 (camera details)."

Figure 8.2 Midjourney generated image of President Obama and Mark Zuckerberg dancing in front of the White House.

Midjourney can create a very realistic-looking fake image that can easily be perceived as accurate if someone doesn't know technology can produce such images (see Figure 8.2).

These capabilities will only grow more robust, and preparing our students for encountering and evaluating questionable content is an urgent responsibility.

CONCLUSION

Educating in the age of AI carries the responsibility of making sure our students are responsible users and intelligent consumers of AI-generated output. Modeling the proper behavior and setting exemplary standards for what is and isn't acceptable will start in our classrooms, and ensuring we have robust policies and procedures in play to help students navigate this new territory is our responsibility.

We also have to prepare students to be mindful of how their actions affect others when they use AI and how they can safeguard themselves from propaganda and misinformation. They also need the foundational knowledge and skills to discuss the ethical implications of AI and advocate for and make decisions that make society safer for everyone.

Teachers can encourage students to critically engage AI by directly incorporating iteration and refining AI content into their classroom assignments, helping students learn the balance between AI and human effort.

In the end, students who can fight misinformation and bias in AI will be critical members of our society who help prevent the instability and threats that malicious actors can create through the misuse of AI.

Exit Ticket

Look through your academic integrity or honesty policy and see if you can modify it to account for AI tools. Make sure not to rely on the ability to detect AI content, and instead create the right classroom culture and provide clear guidance to help students learn responsible usage of AI rather than learn how to subvert school policies.

Chapter 9

Ethical Considerations for AI in Education

The drastic changes AI technology brings to our classrooms and society come with major ethical implications that we must consider before we begin rapidly integrating AI. AI technology was not built primarily for education, and teachers' concerns might differ greatly from those of AI developers.

Many of the major AI companies have articulated their commitment to the ethical development of AI technology. For example, Dave Willner from Trust & Safety at OpenAI says, "In a society where access to generative AI tools will become as essential as access to the internet, we must balance our obligation to mitigate serious risks with allowing diverse values to flourish." Anthropic, a company started by ex-OpenAI employees, has committed to developing "constitutional AI," which they think is safer and more ethical than GPT. Constitutional AI is AI trained on guiding principles rather than specific feedback so that the AI can explicitly learn the values it is supposed to follow rather than implicitly through training. Google, Microsoft, Facebook, and Apple have also committed to developing ethical and responsible AI technologies and tools and carefully self-regulating the technology.

The problem remains that educators will still need to decide the ethical implications and concerns about these technologies absent governmental regulations and policies. Some fundamental concerns revolve around privacy and data collection, as the amount of information that AI companies use to train their models thrives off of more data. While providing AI tools with student data will be essential to many of the features and possibilities outlined in earlier chapters, ensuring that the data is only used for those purposes and that student privacy is respected will be an important consideration in choosing AI tools.

Educators must account for ethical considerations when implementing AI in the classroom. They will need to research and vet tools for their ethical guidelines and values, collaborate with administrators and parents on what values should be adopted, and create critical evaluation processes to ensure that AI tools are only used to help teachers and students improve the learning environment. Educators must also seek professional development to stay updated with new developments and concerns and advocate with their colleagues to ensure companies committed to ethical values act accordingly.

Ethical considerations also revolve around using and accessing AI technologies, even if they meet basic expectations. We need to ensure that implementing AI-driven changes in our classrooms does not further the achievement gap, but helps us make strides toward reducing it. Ensuring equitable access to technology will be critical to ensure that we do not further the digital divide and under prepare a significant chunk of our student population.

Integrating AI technologies will come with major responsibilities for educators, and establishing the right frameworks for thinking about these things now will serve our students and us in the future.

REDUCING, NOT EXPANDING, THE ACHIEVEMENT GAP

- How might AI expand the achievement gap?
- What measures can prevent AI from widening the achievement gap?
- How can AI help close the achievement gap?

Most of this book has outlined AI's current and future transformative potential in education. While all of these benefits are much too great to lament about AI in education, significant risks exist for our most vulnerable students if we do not thoughtfully implement AI in a way that is equitable and tailored toward reducing the gap. AI tools can help our strongest performing students by challenging them, preparing them for successful careers, and playing to their strengths. The risk we face is overemphasizing and prioritizing these benefits over the ones the students that most need individual attention can reap.

We can make multiple mistakes that would make the achievement gap worse rather than better.

Underestimating Bias: It is well established that AI algorithms are biased because of how they are developed and the data sets used to train them. The internet is likely littered with biases, misinformation, and partial data and content that influence the information the AI tools are generating. We need to be careful not to perpetuate these biases by encouraging students to rely on tools that contain them. Instead, we must teach our students what those biases might be, how to identify them explicitly, and how to compensate for them through their own contributions. We must try to advocate for AI tools that are trained to overcome these biases and train ourselves and our students well enough to avoid perpetuating systemic inequities that negatively impact our marginalized students.

Ignoring Accessibility: While AI tools have the potential to make our classrooms more accessible through the various innovations and capabilities that we outlined in earlier chapters, if we do not choose tools that make sure of those capabilities, we will be unable to make good on the potential to make our classrooms more inclusive. Tools must be selected with diversity in mind, and tools that emphasize different learning styles and needs should be prioritized over ones that only cater to a subset of our students, even if it is the majority of them.

Rushing to Higher-Order Thinking: As AI systems handle lower-level thinking skills, we must pursue higher-order thinking skills in our classrooms to ensure our students can keep up with the AI systems and the changes they will bring to our workforce. The danger in focusing on higher-order thinking skills too soon is that the students who need help forming the lower-level ones might use AI as a shortcut to catch up with their classmates. This may lead to students who do not have the foundational critical thinking skills necessary to build stronger, more nuanced thinking skills that classrooms are likely to focus on. We must emphasize the importance of lower-order thinking skills and accurately evaluate our students early on to prevent missing students who need support developing them.

Ignoring Misuse: Schools and educators must stay current with AI technology developments to spot misuse inhibiting students from genuinely learning. Suppose students focus on "gaming the system," and teachers are unaware or are not acting to minimize the potential for circumventing formative activities. In that case, we will have students who are overly reliant on AI for answers and unable to act or think independently.

Banning AI: The initial response from some major school districts, including the New York City Public Schools, was to ban the use of ChatGPT in schools. The biggest loophole in these bans is that students can still access ChatGPT on non-school networks and devices, and affluent students are more likely to have access to these resources. Students learning about AI from other sources are also more likely to know how to circumvent the bans (using different tools that are not banned but produce similar results) and learn how to use AI tools in a way that makes them undetectable. Instead, we must help every student learn how to use AI productively, develop AI literacy, and access AI tools to help them learn and engage rather than reduce workload.

Ignoring AI Literacy: If we ignore AI literacy in schools, it will have some of the same impacts as a ban: some students will become proficient at these technologies on their own, while others will not gain the exposure to be able to operate in an AI-powered world. We will end up limiting future opportunities for those students and increasing the gap between the digitally fluent and digitally naive populations. We must promote AI literacy in schools so all students learn to navigate and benefit from the new tools.

Overrelying on AI: While AI can be built to tailor its experience for personalized learning, we risk over-standardizing the learning our students do if we do not choose tools that specialize in adapting to our students' needs and interests. Suppose we allow algorithms that know nothing about our students to make significant decisions without teacher guidance or student input. In that case, we will limit students' opportunities to explore their strengths and interests and excel uniquely.

Retracting to Standardization: If we respond to the threat of cheating and plagiarism by focusing on rapid testing and quizzing in classrooms, we are likely to perpetuate the fractures in our education system rather than solve them. AI allows us to rethink how we teach and what we make students learn. Instead of embracing the potential for radical change, if we resort to pop quizzes and more tests, we will continue to grow the achievement gap and further reduce student engagement.

Forgetting about Humans: Throughout the book, I've emphasized that humanity will remain a key component of our education systems. Our students need empathy, emotional support, and a nuanced understanding of their lives and situations to grow and flourish. If we rely so much on AI systems that schooling begins to lack the human touch, we will eliminate an element crucial for students who may already be struggling. We must continue working closely with our students and use AI tools as a complement, not a replacement.

Undertraining Teachers: Teacher support and professional development is already abysmal and have contributed to the teacher burnout and flight crisis. If we do not support our teachers during this monumental change, we will leave behind entire classrooms full of students who will not have teachers equipped with the knowledge or resources to help them navigate the new era. Teachers will be unaware of or unable to respond to the changes, and our teachers and students in the most underserved areas will most likely suffer if we do not prioritize universal training for teachers.

As we continue to work on integrating AI into our schools, we should consistently remember to evaluate AI's impact on student outcomes with a focus on the achievement gap. If we are mindful of the preceding concerns and use consistent feedback loops to adjust our strategies, we are more likely to benefit our students during the age of AI rather than harm them.

AI, if used thoughtfully, can aid in bridging the achievement gap. We've shown examples of robust differentiation, personalization, identification of struggling students, and data-driven decision-making as areas where AI can contribute to equitable outcomes. We need to do our part in making the most of those capabilities for the growth of our students.

We must encourage collaboration among educators, administrators, and students to create robust, equity-focused strategies for

AI use in schools. With careful implementation and an equity and student-focused approach, AI can be a valuable tool in reducing the achievement gap.

ADDRESSING THE DIGITAL DIVIDE AND ENSURING ACCESS

- What are the risks of ignoring the digital divide?
- What strategies can be used to ensure all students have access to AI tools?
- How can schools help bridge the digital divide?

The digital divide has already added to the achievement gap problem by limiting students' access to the necessary tools and information to support them. Technology has already been playing an important role in modern education, and the pandemic only grew the reliance of our classrooms on technology to deliver effective and engaging instruction.

The introduction of AI will further necessitate access to technology as we begin to rely on their help for personalized instruction. We must be diligent about narrowing the disparity between those who can access technology and those who cannot, especially before a further divide is created between those who have access to AI tools and those who do not. Thus, we must think proactively about reducing the existing digital divide and preventing a future one.

If we ignore the digital divide, we are likely to widen the achievement gap along socioeconomic lines, with students from affluent families and neighborhoods continuing to have better access to future opportunities. As more and more industries adopt AI, the students who are not exposed to AI tools and technology, in general, will have reduced career prospects, thus perpetuating intergenerational poverty. Students without access to the new tools will also continue to showcase reduced engagement and motivation in schools and not have the appropriate tools to get custom, tailored interventions from AI systems.

We risk further marginalizing these students as teachers struggle to teach digital literacy without digital access and themselves face hurdles and challenges that could be reduced by increasing access to digital devices. All of this will lead to subsets of our population that are unprepared and technologically illiterate for the AI-driven workforce.

Schools need to start by ensuring equitable access to existing tools. We need to continue to build infrastructure for one-to-one devices, reliable internet access, access to the latest software and tools, and training and support for teachers and students to effectively use all of these things. Schools should ensure that AI tools that are implemented are either low-cost or free to the students and provide programs for subsidizing access for students who otherwise would not be able to make use of the technological developments. Teachers should be given plenty of professional development to empower and support their students as they learn new technologies.

Schools should also look to partner with local communities to increase access to resources outside of school. For example, schools can work with libraries to provide access to AI tools on their computers and offer training and support to parents and students. Schools can also seek tools that work on lower bandwidth networks and work from mobile devices to increase access for students with limited resources.

Until the digital divide can be bridged, teachers should continue to offer blended learning and technology-independent options that are just as robust for learning to avoid alienating or marginalizing students.

If we can act sooner rather than later, we can prepare our communities to ensure access to the digital tools needed to prepare students for the age of AI and avoid playing catch-up once we rely more on AI tools. The rapid pace of technology development makes the call to action for reducing the digital divide more urgent than ever, and teachers play an influential role in advocating on behalf of their students to ensure we promote and realize digital equity.

PROTECTING STUDENT PRIVACY AND DATA SECURITY

- What are the key privacy concerns related to AI in education?
- How can schools ensure student data security when using AI tools?
- What role do parents/guardians and students play in protecting student privacy?

The thing that makes AI tools valuable complements to our classrooms is the same thing that threatens our students the most. The amount of data needed to train and run AI systems opens the possibility for exploitation and privacy leaks that jeopardize and unfairly take advantage of our students.

Technology companies already collect enormous amounts of data on us and our students. Most of our online interactions are monitored and tracked, whether it be our search history, emails, online presence, or videos we watch. AI tools will collect even more data as they get first-hand access to our conversations, classrooms, and students. This data can be exploited for use in training without the informed consent of the students and teachers or for commercial purposes like targeted advertising. These companies could also share student data with third parties, including colleges, major corporations, insurance companies, or whomever they can sell the data to if the right policies and regulations are not implemented.

The data could also be used for surveillance and student profiling, even by schools themselves, which goes against basic privacy principles. This could be used to identify students likely to have behavioral issues, determine which students a district accepts, or inform law enforcement about students who "may" run into trouble. These actions are highly contentious, at the least, and educators and schools should be careful in how they approach the data being collected and shared.

The existence of large pools of data also makes them vulnerable to data breaches and leaked data to bad actors, even if the company doesn't intentionally share or misuse data. Where and how long data is stored impact how safe AI systems will be for our students and teachers.

In response to these threats, schools and teachers need to implement the following measures:

- **Develop standards:** Only choose companies that contractually promise not to share data or use it for commercial purposes, and have industry standard encryption and other security measures.

- **Vet vendors:** Choose vendors who have a history of working with educators and have a track record of being reliable and trustworthy.

- **Conduct audits:** Regularly check in with the AI companies being used on any potential security vulnerabilities, breaches, and changes in best practices to avoid issues.

- **Limit data:** Choose tools that only collect the data necessary to provide the desired services and do not collect data just for collection.

- **Train staff:** Teachers should be trained on how to spot issues, how to help students avoid oversharing details, and how to communicate with parents and guardians about necessary information.

Parents and students should also be involved in the process to help ensure all stakeholders are on the same page about the schools' commitment to privacy:

- **Seek informed consent:** Make sure that parents are aware of all tools being used and offer them the opportunity to ask about data collection practices.

- **Educate parents:** Provide parents with information on how to help students protect their privacy at home.

- **Engage students:** Work with students to develop digital citizenship skills so that they are empowered to advocate for and protect their own safety.

If these steps are taken, and companies are held accountable for maximizing student safety, schools can incorporate AI technologies into their classrooms without risking harming their students. We have to remember that we already accept some level of risk from technology companies with the tools we allow students to use, and we should continue to be mindful of exercising caution across the board. However, we should also acknowledge that the opportunity to serve our students better requires ethical data collection and prioritizing the right privacy and security measures rather than avoiding implementing new solutions.

CONCLUSION

In conclusion, the ethical implications of AI technology in education present a complex challenge. Our classrooms and society stand at the cusp of a transformation shaped by this technology. While we should be excited to embrace the full potential of AI, we need to be thoughtful and deliberate in our approach to ensure it aligns with our ethical principles.

While AI companies are trying to be proactive about the impact of their technologies on society, the ultimate responsibility is for educators to consider the nuances of the various technologies and the contexts in which we integrate them to ensure safety for all our students.

We must continue to be mindful of how data is shared with third parties and ensure that student and teacher privacy is respected. We must also work together to identify changes we need to make to our educational system to most effectively embrace the age of AI without worsening existing problems. We have to ensure that the benefits of AI help us reach the students who need us most rather than letting them fall behind as we integrate new technologies.

Ethical considerations for AI integration in the classroom require a proactive approach, and meeting these challenges will ensure that the promise of AI in education is effectively realized for all.

Exit Ticket

Take this opportunity to formally articulate your values and commitments as you integrate AI into your classroom. What are your guiding principles? What harms are you going to be more vigilant about? How will you avoid harming your students as you embrace the potential of AI?

Chapter **10**

Teacher Professional Development in the AI Era

Professional development has always been an important cornerstone of teachers' careers by helping them stay up-to-date and engaged with the latest trends in educational theory. It has also been a tedious and cumbersome task for some as the quality of professional development is inconsistent and often is offered during periods of time that are inconvenient for teachers.

As technology evolves, teachers will need to consider further pedagogical integrations to continue using the latest innovations. We hope that schools and districts will recognize the increased need for professional development and provide teachers with the necessary support and resources to support ongoing professional development with AI and education. More than ever, teachers will need workshops, seminars, and training sessions to discuss best practices and learn new innovative techniques and strategies. They will also need support evaluating tools and platforms and help to form policies and guidelines.

While AI will increase the need for professional development, as new technologies and trends develop rapidly and require teachers to stay current with educational theory and technological changes, not all of the implications will be bad. AI will also offer new avenues for teachers to pursue professional development and help them iterate on their teaching practice quicker and more effectively.

THE IMPORTANCE OF CONTINUED ADAPTATION AND GROWTH

- Why is adaptability important for educators in the age of AI?
- How can educators foster a growth mindset in their own professional lives?
- How can schools support educators in their journey of professional growth?

The preceding chapters and the range of capabilities and possibilities make clear that the education landscape will continue to evolve in the coming years. This requires teachers to rapidly adapt to new tools, methods, and strategies.

Teachers will need to stay current on the advancement to make the most of the technology in their practice and ensure they are preparing students for the world as it will be. They will also need to stay current on best practices regarding ethics, privacy, and security and avoid any issues that may cause further digital inequity among their students.

In order to model the same growth mindset that they will have to instill in their students, teachers will have to adapt their teaching practices and resources as new innovations emerge. For example, teachers will likely have to make these changes during the school year rather than wait until the summer to integrate a new tool or adapt an assignment to avoid new cheating tools.

Teachers will need to prioritize thinking about how they continuously learn, whether through formal opportunities like courses and conferences or informal ones like webinars and books. They will need to see the changes as opportunities for growth and development, and expect and anticipate that there will be obstacles during the school year.

Teachers should regularly reflect on their own teaching experience and seek feedback from their peers and students to collaborate on new developments, best practices, and tips and tricks that can be shared together. While we don't want to treat the classroom completely like a laboratory, we will have to be open to experimenting with new approaches and tools and learning from our successes and failures what our own teaching styles are in the age of AI.

Teachers must also take care of themselves! The age of AI should begin to make our lives easier, not harder. Focus on prioritizing self-care and remember that everyone is adapting to the new changes simultaneously. The key is to keep learning, innovating, and adapting to ensure you become the best practitioner you can be.

Schools will need to provide the necessary support to empower them to take advantage of the opportunities. They will need to allocate funding toward tools, provide and support professional development opportunities, and offer space for collaboration among colleagues. They will also need to support experiments and recognize and reward teachers who innovate successfully.

All of these things can help teachers form the right habits and mindsets to survive teaching in the age of AI and thrive in it.

ESSENTIAL AI COMPETENCIES FOR EDUCATORS

- What are the core AI competencies for educators?

- What skills and practices do educators need to be AI literate?

- How can educators build a strong foundation to withstand future change?

While this book aims to serve as a primer for teachers to form core competencies, teachers will need to seek further development based on their own interests and needs. The core competencies to think about teaching in the age of AI are:

- **AI basics:** Teachers will need to retain the foundational information about AI technology, such as machine learning, natural language processing, and neural networks.

- **Data literacy:** Data will increasingly play a larger role in how we think about education, and the ability to navigate and make sense of analytics that AI systems generate will be a necessary skill set.

- **Ethical considerations:** As the integration of AI continues, new ethical considerations may become apparent that will require educators to think critically about and navivate.

- **Pedagogical integration:** The ability to effectively incorporate new AI tools into teaching practices and strategies will ensure the effort is well spent.

- **AI tool evaluation:** New AI tools are coming out every day, and teachers will need to be able to sort through the noise to evaluate them for relevance, efficacy, and alignment with their own objectives.

- **Communication:** As teachers incorporate AI into their instructional practice, they will need to communicate with parents and administrators about the changes they are making.

- **Technical proficiency:** Teachers will be the first technical support line for many students, and the more digitally literate they are, the more they can support their students.

Teachers will need to incorporate various methods into their professional development for integrating AI into education. Teachers should try to incorporate:

- **Events:** Workshops, webinars, and conferences offer a great way for teachers to quickly see what is new and gain actionable insight.
- **Courses:** Online courses, in-person classes, and MOOCs on AI and education and even just AI can help teachers build a robust foundation of knowledge.
- **Reading:** Subscribing to newsletters, blogs, and journals will allow teachers to gain bite-sized information about AI as it comes out.
- **Networking:** Connecting with other educators on social media, forums, and in-person seminars will provide opportunities to exchange ideas and learn from other teachers.

While these suggestions are not unique to AI, they can remind teachers of the resources available to navigate these new changes.

We offer many of these resources on our website (pedagog.ai), including an accredited course, weekly newsletter, online events, and a forum for teachers to exchange ideas. We also regularly share resources for teachers to engage in professional development on our social media channels!

LEVERAGING AI FOR PERSONAL AND PROFESSIONAL DEVELOPMENT

- How can educators use AI tools to support educators' personal and professional growth?

- How can educators use AI for professional development now?
- How might educators be able to use AI for professional development in the future?

Throughout the book, we have provided examples of AI that students and educators can use to enhance student learning. Many of those same tactics and tools can be used by teachers themselves to direct their own learning.

AI tools offer a great way for teachers to find personalized learning resources and lessons based on their own interests, strengths, and areas for improvement. For example, you can input feedback from a review and ask an AI bot to help you improve in an area of weakness.

The same tools can also help you think through your own classroom practices, suggest new innovative strategies for you to try, and even read through your work and provide feedback. Using AI tools in your learning journey will also better equip you to support students on their learning journeys.

As AI tools become further integrated, they will be able to provide feedback based on classroom interactions, help you role-play teaching in virtual reality classrooms, and suggest changes and adaptations based on your own teaching style. You will be able to record your class and submit it to an AI tool for analysis or even use a virtual coach to help provide personalized guidance, support, and mentoring.

For now, you can use your own insight and external feedback to seek the right resources and make a plan to grow as an educator.

Prompt It!

- **Self-Evaluation:** "Help me conduct a self-evaluation of my teaching techniques."
- **Journal:** "Provide some journal prompts to help me reflect on my teaching style."

- **New Strategies:** "Share innovative teaching strategies to engage students in a {fill} class."

- **Differentiation:** "Describe some strategies for differentiating instruction to meet the diverse needs of my students."

- **Self-Care:** "What are some effective strategies for stress management and self-care as a teacher?"

- **Bloom's Taxonomy:** "How can I effectively apply Bloom's Taxonomy in developing my lesson plans?"

- **Flipped Classroom:** "How can the flipped classroom model enhance student learning in a high school math class?"

- **Inquiry-Based Learning:** "Provide examples of inquiry-based learning activities for a middle school science class."

- **Socratic Method:** "How can I best utilize the Socratic method in a high school literature class?"

- **AI:** "Suggest ways to incorporate AI tools in a high school physics curriculum."

- **Incorporating Feedback:** "A colleague observed that my instructions can sometimes be confusing. How can I improve the clarity of my instructions?"

- **Tips:** "How can I improve my public speaking skills for leading teacher training workshops?"

CONCLUSION

As we continue into the age of AI, the significance of professional development for teachers will only continue to grow. The fast pace and dramatic overhaul will necessitate similarly fast-paced and robust professional development for teachers. Developing foundational AI mastery will help teachers integrate these tools effectively and impart the necessary skills to their students.

School districts will have to play a large role in ensuring that they are facilitating the enhanced need for professional development and working with teachers to provide them with the appropriate resources.

However, the capability of AI to support learning can make professional development less of a chore and more of a personalized experience for teachers too. It can offer innovative ways for educators to enhance their pedagogical approaches and adapt their teaching to better meet their students' needs. In doing so, AI will not only be helping our students learn, but also guiding teachers along their own learning journeys.

Exit Ticket

Make a plan to pursue further professional development in AI in education. Find relevant newsletters, blogs, online events, and courses, and commit to following up on the latest trends and developments using various methods. Try to make a robust plan and see if you can form a working group with fellow colleagues to keep each other accountable!

Chapter 11

Adapting and Growing with AI in Education

One thing I hope is clear from this book is that education will not look the same ever again. After the Covid-19 pandemic, we faced massive challenges and educational changes that we overcame together as a community. However, many of those changes were short-lived, and most of education has returned to the same practices and strategies used before the pandemic. This challenge is not the same. We will never be able to return to education as we knew it before the invention of the latest AI technologies, and it is in our and our students' best interests if we embrace these changes and learn to adapt and grow with AI.

While I do not consider the challenges posed by AI for our society insignificant, I also do not believe they are insurmountable. If we continue to ground our decisions and actions in our values as a community and the reality of the external world, I truly believe that we can continue to serve our students in ways that prepare them for whatever the future holds for us.

What I do think would be a mistake is to ignore or avoid confronting the challenges until it is too late. We cannot afford to lose more time than we already have in changing our educational systems and environments to be more conducive to supporting the level of technological integration that has become possible. There are clear areas where our education system has shortcomings in serving our students, and this is a perfect opportunity to address those head-on.

Trying to ban or prevent the use of AI in our classrooms and society will be a lost cause. Just as I finish this book, New York City Public Schools lifted their ChatGPT ban. The Chancellor announced the lift in the ban by saying, "the knee-jerk fear and risk overlooked the potential of generative AI to support students and teachers, as well as the reality that our students are participating in and will work in a world where understanding generative AI is crucial." On the same day, OpenAI released an iPhone application for ChatGPT, further increasing the accessibility of the generative AI bot.

These changes in both technology and policy will continue to operate at these speeds, and while we may have had months or years to react to changes before, we may have weeks or days to react or risk losing valuable time with our students to prepare them for the world outside our classrooms.

We must all operate with the mentality that AI will continue progressing along the stages of development outlined in Chapter 2, and prepare ourselves and our students for the age of AI by embracing the mindset shifts outlined in Chapter 3.

Chapters 4–7 outlined how AI systems are making our dreams as a community come true. We will be able to differentiate and personalize education in ways we never thought possible while freeing up our own time to further provide students with the care and support they need to grow into empathetic and well-rounded individuals. We will have the power to assess our students more quickly and accurately, support their personal learning goals, and meet our own objectives with much more efficacy. Our classrooms will become truly inclusive sites of joyful learning, and our time will be spent doing what we do best: teaching.

Many of the changes outlined in the book might take years to come into all our classrooms, but it's important to realize that every single change that is mentioned in this book is possible now. There is likely at least one teacher or student in the world making use of the technology in the ways I have suggested we ought to use on a broader scale.

There are also technologies that I have not mentioned that are not likely to be implemented or are impracticable at scale right now. They still highlight the potential of AI in education. For example, classrooms in China are experimenting with headbands that use AI to monitor students' attention and focus to help teachers identify students drifting from instruction. Similarly, as other technological advancements such as virtual and augmented reality, the Internet of Things, and the metaverse combine with AI, we will likely continue to see more unique educational innovations.

The signs all point to a dramatically different society inside and outside our school buildings. We will need to continue growing together and learning from each other as we develop new strategies, tools, theories, and practices.

We will also need to empower our students to navigate these changes themselves. Chapter 8 outlines how our students will need the skills to use these technologies, protect themselves from the malicious actors who manipulate the technologies to harm others, and contribute meaningfully to society side-by-side as AI technologies take on greater shares of the workload.

We also need to work together to ensure that these tools are implemented in ways that protect our students. As Chapter 9 outlines, making existing equity problems worse or creating new issues with data and privacy would hinder the progress possible with AI. We can solve many of our biggest problems by integrating AI, but we must be thoughtful and intentional to do so without creating other ones.

As AI handles more and more of the routine tasks that make up our day, there will be a shift in the roles of educators. We will be able to focus more on mentoring, guidance, higher-order thinking, and relationship-building with our students. Chapter 10 provides some ways educators can continue adapting to these changes with the right resources and tools.

All of these developments will enable us to help our students grow into individuals who can flourish as lifelong learners with the right skills and dispositions to live meaningful lives with those around them. It is certain that teaching will always play a central role in our society, but what and how we teach will never look the same again in the age of AI.

Acknowledgments

This book is the product of a collective effort, and there are some individuals I must acknowledge.

To my parents, Jalpa and Hiten Shah, thank you for instilling in me the value of education, a virtue I have cherished and tried to uphold.

My siblings, Chandani and Kasish Shah, have been my first pupils and intellectual sparring partners. Your readiness to engage with, learn from, and challenge my thoughts has been integral to my growth. Kirk Aleman, my older brother, has been my sounding board and my motivational coach. Your friendship, your honesty, and your insights have been invaluable in this endeavor.

My deepest appreciation goes to my partner, Sitara Soundararajan. Your unwavering support and ability to help me articulate my thoughts have been a source of immense strength and courage.

I am deeply indebted to my editor, Ashante Thomas, for her tireless efforts in pulling together this project. Thank you for your quick work in making this book happen. Your swift and smart actions have been a game-changer.

I extend my gratitude to my teachers and professors. Your mentorship extended beyond the realm of the classroom walls — you taught me not just facts and figures, but also how to truly appreciate education.

Last but not least, my sincerest gratitude to my team at Peda-gogy.Cloud. You have made the impossible possible, and in times of need, you have been more than colleagues, you have been my family. I would like to extend a special thanks to Nina Bamberg, who has been an immense support, holding down the fort as I focused on this book. Your dedication, commitment, and loyalty are matchless.

To everyone who has been a part of this journey, thank you. This book is a product of your support and belief.

About the Author

Priten Shah is a serial entrepreneur whose projects aim to drive change and innovation in education. Priten has an MEd in Education Policy and Management from Harvard Graduate School of Education and a BA in Philosophy from Harvard College.

Priten has had the privilege of educating a wide array of students, ranging from language schools in South Korea to special education classes in New York. These diverse classroom experiences have been instrumental in his understanding of students' unique needs, fostering his ability to deliver tailored educational solutions.

A believer in the transformative power of technology, Priten has spearheaded numerous groundbreaking projects, including designing custom Learning Management Systems, developing gamified learning applications, and creating mastery-learning-based online courses.

He currently runs two education ventures: United 4 Social Change (U4SC) and Pedagogy.Cloud.

At U4SC, his focus is on fostering healthier democracies through interdisciplinary education, making civics education accessible to all. U4SC helps teachers integrate civics into their curricula through animated videos, lesson plans, and innovative classroom activities.

Pedagogy.Cloud, on the other hand, blends his passion for education with the latest technology. He and his team are helping educators keep pace with rapid advancements in AI. Their projects include a customizable chatbot for teachers to use in their classrooms (Socrat. ai) and professional development resources and curriculum development tools for teachers (Pedagog.ai).

In all his endeavors, Priten remains steadfast in his mission: driving innovative solutions to meet the diverse and intricate needs of learners in a rapidly evolving world. His ultimate vision is straightforward yet ambitious — ensuring we are all Prepared for a Dynamic Tomorrow.

Index

Page numbers followed by *f* refer to figures.

Newsletters, creating, 143, 145f–146f
New York City Public Schools, 201–202, 219

O

OpenAI, 198, 219
Open-endedness, of prompts, 27
Oral presentation topics, creating, 120
Outlining, 193
Output layers, of artificial neural networks, 20
Overreliance, on AI, 202

P

Pace, of learning, 166
Paperwork, 153–157
Parents:
    communication with, 137–138, 143, 144f
    and data security, 208
    involving, in teaching digital citizenship, 188
    prompts for communicating with, 147
Pedagogy, 51–89
    active learning, 61–64
    behaviorist theory, 56–58
    Bloom's Taxonomy, 69–76
    constructivist theory, 53–56
    differentiated instruction, 76–80
    fostering collaboration and relationship-building, 81–84
    inquiry-based learning, 84–88
    integrating AI into, 213
    problem- and project-based learning, 64–69
    sociocultural theory, 58–60

Peer-to-peer interactions, 177
Performance tasks, 123
Permission slips, creating, 154–155, 155f–156f
Personal development, 214–216
Personalized content, 77, 78
Personalized learning:
    in active learning classrooms, 61
    created by AI, 25–26
    in knowledge construction, 54
    in problem- and project-based learning, 65
Personalized learning pathways, 71, 77, 133, 165–168
Photos, AI-generated, 195–196, 196f
Plagiarism, 1, 23
Portfolio creation guides, creating, 120
Presentations, creating with AI, 110, 111f
Privacy, 182, 183, 206–208
Problem-based learning, 64–69, 71
Problem sets, creating, 118
Problem-solving skills:
    developing, 38
    and growth mindset, 44
    importance of, 37
    in knowledge construction, 54
    using real-world problems for, 48
Professional development, 210–217
    essential AI competencies, 213–214
    importance of continued adaptation and growth, 211–212
    leveraging AI for personal and, 214–216
    for using AI, 29